THE BAZI 60 PILLARS
LIFE ANALYSIS METHOD

一柱論命法

XIN
Yin Metal
PILLARS

The BaZi 60 Pillars Life Analysis Method - Xin Metal

Copyright © 2013 by Joey Yap
All rights reserved worldwide.
First Edition February 2013
2nd Print August 2013

All intellectual property rights contained or in relation to this book belongs to Joey Yap.

No part of this book may be copied, used, subsumed, or exploited in fact, field of thought or general idea, by any other authors or persons, or be stored in a retrieval system, transmitted or reproduced in any way, including but not limited to digital copying and printing in any form whatsoever worldwide without the prior agreement and written permission of the author.

The author can be reached at:

Joey Yap Research International Sdn. Bhd. (939831- H)
19-3, The Boulevard, Mid Valley City,
59200 Kuala Lumpur, Malaysia.
Tel   : +603-2284 8080
Fax   : +603-2284 1218
Email   : info@masteryacademy.com
Website : www.masteryacademy.com

DISCLAIMER:

The author, Joey Yap and the publisher, JY Productions Sdn Bhd, have made their best efforts to produce this high quality, informative and helpful book. They have verified the technical accuracy of the information and contents of this book. Any information pertaining to the events, occurrences, dates and other details relating to the person or persons, dead or alive, and to the companies have been verified to the best of their abilities based on information obtained or extracted from various websites, newspaper clippings and other public media. However, they make no representation or warranties of any kind with regard to the contents of this book and accept no liability of any kind for any losses or damages caused or alleged to be caused directly or indirectly from using the information contained herein.

Published by JY Productions Sdn. Bhd. (944330-D)

INDEX

1	**Introduction**	13
2	**Xin 辛 (Yin Metal)**	53
3	**DI TIAN SUI 滴天髓**	56
4	**Xin Metal According to Di Tian Sui 滴天髓**	57
5	**Xin Chou 辛丑 (Metal Ox)**	61
	• **Getting to Know Xin Chou 辛丑 (Metal Ox)**	63
	• **Work Life**	69
	• **Love and Relationships**	73
	• **Technical Analysis 67**	79
	• **Unique 60 Pillar Combinations**	85
	Heaven Combine Earth Punish 天合地刑 **Xin Chou 辛丑** (Metal Ox) + **Bing Xu 丙戌** (Fire Dog)	86
	Heaven Combine Earth Harm 天合地害 **Xin Chou 辛丑** (Metal Ox) + **Bing Wu 丙午** (Fire Horse)	88
	Heaven Friend Earth Clash 天比地沖 **Xin Chou 辛丑** (Metal Ox) + **Xin Wei 辛未** (Metal Goat)	90
	Heaven and Earth Clash 天沖地沖 **Xin Chou 辛丑** (Metal Ox) + **Ding Wei 丁未** (Fire Goat)	92
	Heaven Counter Earth Clash 天剋地沖 **Xin Chou 辛丑** (Metal Ox) + **Yi Wei 乙未** (Wood Goat)	94
	Heaven and Earth Unity 天同地比 **Xin Chou 辛丑** (Metal Ox) + **Xin Chou 辛丑** (Metal Ox)	96
	Heaven and Earth Combine 天地相合 **Xin Chou 辛丑** (Metal Ox) + **Bing Zi 丙子** (Fire Rat)	98
	Rob Wealth Goat Blade 劫財羊刃 **Xin Chou 辛丑** (Metal Ox) + **Geng Xu 庚戌** (Metal Dog)	100

6 Xin Mao 辛卯 (Metal Rabbit) — 103

- **Getting to Know Xin Mao 辛卯 (Metal Rabbit)** — 105
- **Work Life** — 111
- **Love and Relationships** — 115
- **Technical Analysis** — 119
- **Unique 60 Pillar Combinations** — 125

Na Yin Death and Extinct 納音死絕 Xin Mao 辛卯 (Metal Rabbit) + Bing Shen 丙申 (Fire Monkey)	126
Heaven Combine Earth Punish 天合地刑 Xin Mao 辛卯 (Metal Rabbit) + Bing Zi 丙子 (Fire Rat)	128
Heaven Combine Earth Harm 天合地害 Xin Mao 辛卯 (Metal Rabbit) + Bing Chen 丙辰 (Fire Dragon)	130
Heaven Friend Earth Clash 天比地沖 Xin Mao 辛卯 (Metal Rabbit) + Xin You 辛酉 (Metal Rooster)	132
Heaven and Earth Clash 天沖地沖 Xin Mao 辛卯 (Metal Rabbit) + Ding You 丁酉 (Fire Rooster)	136
Heaven Counter Earth Clash 天剋地沖 Xin Mao 辛卯 (Metal Rabbit) + Yi You 乙酉 (Earth Rooster)	138
Heaven and Earth Unity 天同地比 Xin Mao 辛卯 (Metal Rabbit) + Xin Mao 辛卯 (Metal Rabbit)	140
Heaven and Earth Combine 天地相合 Xin Mao 辛卯 (Metal Rabbit) + Bing Xu 丙戌 (Fire Dog)	142
Mutual Exchange Goat Blade 互換羊刃 Xin Mao 辛卯 (Metal Rabbit) + Jia Xu 甲戌 (Wood Dog)	144
Rob Wealth Goat Blade 劫財羊刃 Xin Mao 辛卯 (Metal Rabbit) + Geng Xu 庚戌 (Metal Dog)	145

7	**Xin Si** 辛巳 (Metal Snake)	147
	• Getting to Know Xin Si 辛巳 (Metal Snake)	149
	• Work Life	155
	• Love and Relationships	159
	• Technical Analysis	163
	• Unique 60 Pillar Combinations	169
	Heaven Combine Earth Punish 天合地刑 **Xin Si** 辛巳 (Metal Snake) + **Bing Shen** 丙申 (Fire Monkey)	170
	Heaven Combine Earth Harm 天合地害 **Xin Si** 辛巳 (Metal Snake) + **Bing Yin** 丙寅 (Fire Tiger)	172
	Heaven Friend Earth Clash 天比地冲 **Xin Si** 辛巳 (Metal Snake) + **Xin Hai** 辛亥 (Metal Pig)	174
	Heaven and Earth Clash 天冲地冲 **Xin Si** 辛巳 (Metal Snake) + **Ding Hai** 丁亥 (Fire Pig)	176
	Heaven Counter Earth Clash 天尅地冲 **Xin Si** 辛巳 (Metal Snake) + **Yi Hai** 乙亥 (Wood Pig)	178
	Heaven and Earth Unity 天同地比 **Xin Si** 辛巳 (Metal Snake) + **Xin Si** 辛巳 (Metal Snake)	180
	Heaven and Earth Combine 天地相合 **Xin Si** 辛巳 (Metal Snake) + **Bing Shen** 丙申 (Fire Monkey)	182
	Rob Wealth Goat Blade 劫財羊刃 **Xin Si** 辛巳 (Metal Snake) + **Geng Xu** 庚戌 (Metal Dog)	184

8	Xin Wei 辛未 (Metal Goat)	187
	• Getting to Know Xin Wei 辛未 (Metal Goat)	189
	• Work Life	195
	• Love and Relationships	199
	• Technical Analysis	205
	• Unique 60 Pillar Combinations	211
	Heaven Combine Earth Punish 天合地刑 Xin Wei 辛未 (Metal Goat) + Bing Xu 丙戌 (Fire Dog)	212
	Heaven Combine Earth Harm 天合地害 Xin Wei 辛未 (Metal Goat) + Bing Zi 丙子 (Fire Rat)	216
	Heaven Friend Earth Clash 天比地冲 Xin Wei 辛未 (Metal Goat) + Xin Chou 辛丑 (Metal Ox)	218
	Heaven and Earth Clash 天冲地冲 Xin Wei 辛未 (Metal Goat) + Ding Chou 丁丑 (Fire Ox)	220
	Heaven Counter Earth Clash 天剋地冲 Xin Wei 辛未 (Metal Goat) + Yi Chou 乙丑 (Wood Ox)	222
	Heaven and Earth Unity 天同地比 Xin Wei 辛未 (Metal Goat) + Xin Wei 辛未 (Metal Goat)	224
	Heaven and Earth Combine 天地相合 Xin Wei 辛未 (Metal Goat) + Bing Wu 丙午 (Fire Horse)	226
	Rob Wealth Goat Blade 劫財羊刃 Xin Wei 辛未 (Metal Goat) + Geng Xu 庚戌 (Metal Dog)	228

| 9 | **Xin You 辛酉 (Metal Rooster)** | 231 |

- **Getting to Know Xin You 辛酉 (Metal Rooster)** — 233
- **Work Life** — 239
- **Love and Relationships** — 243
- **Technical Analysis** — 247
- **Unique 60 Pillar Combinations** — 253

  - **Na Yin Death and Extinct 納音死絕** — 254
    Xin You 辛酉 (Metal Rooster) + Bing Wu 丙午 (Fire Horse)

  - **Heaven Combine Earth Harm 天合地害** — 256
    Xin You 辛酉 (Metal Rooster) + Bing Xu 丙戌 (Fire Dog)

  - **Heaven Friend Earth Clash 天比地沖** — 258
    Xin You 辛酉 (Metal Rooster) + Xin Mao 辛卯 (Metal Rabbit)

  - **Heaven and Earth Clash 天沖地沖** — 260
    Xin You 辛酉 (Metal Rooster) + Ding Mao 丁卯 (Fire Rabbit)

  - **Heaven Counter Earth Clash 天剋地沖** — 262
    Xin You 辛酉 (Metal Rooster) + Yi Mao 乙卯 (Wood Rabbit)

  - **Heaven and Earth Unity 天同地比** — 264
    Xin You 辛酉 (Metal Rooster) + Xin You 辛酉 (Metal Rooster)

  - **Heaven and Earth Combine 天地相合** — 266
    Xin You 辛酉 (Metal Rooster) + Bing Chen 丙辰 (Fire Dragon)

  - **Heaven Friend Earth Punish 天比地刑** — 268
    Xin You 辛酉 (Metal Rooster) + Xin You 辛酉 (Metal Rooster)

  - **Mutual Exchange Goat Blade 互換羊刃** — 272
    Xin You 辛酉 (Metal Rooster) + Geng Xu 庚戌 (Metal Dog)

  - **Rob Wealth Goat Blade 劫財羊刃** — 273
    Xin You 辛酉 (Metal Rooster) + Geng Xu 庚戌 (Metal Dog)

10	**Xin Hai 辛亥 (Metal Pig)**	275
	• **Getting to Know Xin Hai 辛亥 (Metal Pig)**	277
	• **Work Life**	283
	• **Love and Relationships**	287
	• **Technical Analysis**	293
	• **Unique 60 Pillar Combinations**	301
	Heaven Combine Earth Harm 天合地害 Xin Hai 辛亥 (Metal Pig) + Bing Shen 丙申 (Fire Monkey)	302
	Heaven Friend Earth Clash 天比地沖 Xin Hai 辛亥 (Metal Pig) + Xin Si 辛巳 (Metal Snake)	304
	Heaven Friend Earth Punish 天比地刑 Xin Hai 辛亥 (Metal Pig) + Xin Hai 辛亥 (Metal Pig)	306
	Heaven and Earth Clash 天沖地沖 Xin Hai 辛亥 (Metal Pig) + Ding Si 丁巳 (Fire Snake)	308
	Heaven Counter Earth Clash 天剋地沖 Xin Hai 辛亥 (Metal Pig) + Yi Si 乙巳 (Wood Snake)	310
	Heaven and Earth Unity 天同地比 Xin Hai 辛亥 (Metal Pig) + Xin Hai 辛亥 (Metal Pig)	312
	Heaven and Earth Combine 天地相合 Xin Hai 辛亥 (Metal Pig) + Bing Yin 丙寅 (Fire Tiger)	314
	Rob Wealth Goat Blade 劫財羊刃 Xin Hai 辛亥 (Metal Pig) + Geng Xu 庚戌 (Metal Dog)	316

Preface

In the past, even the most gifted BaZi students had a hard time getting to grips with the BaZi 60 Pillars. As some of my long time students may recall, the topic was originally covered in Module 4 of my BaZi Mastery program. I was often told that it would be wise to give the topic greater coverage and attention. When I upgraded the BaZi Mastery syllabus back in 2009, I decided that the best thing to do would be to cover the 60 Pillars exclusively in a *new* series of books - one of which you are reading now!

When I first began writing this series, I had no idea what I'd let myself in for. I had to call upon a lifetime of personal study and research, refer to classical interpretation and records and leverage all my years of BaZi Chart assessment and interpretation experience to get the job done. Most pressingly, because this book is intended for the average user of BaZi with little or no BaZi academic background, I had to condense and simplify my findings so that they would be easily understood. This, was hard.

I found the basic, technical elements of this writing process straight-forward. Accurately streamlining, condensing and translating the material from the original records took me a long time, however, and the greatest difficulty was to make sure that my translations and interpretations didn't deviate from or dilute the source material in any meaningful way.

I knew when writing this series that it was important to present the BaZi 60 Pillars in a practical way. This means I had to remove many of the rhetoric technical jargon. In the course of my work as a BaZi consultant, I've dealt with many leaders, businessmen, decision makers and visionaries as well as countless students and enthusiasts, too. One thing I have found in all my dealings is that people do not have the time to make use of the technical, classic-referencing BaZi information in the modern world. They want quick, accurate information which they can use to make decisions, motivate and influence others. Without some kind of intermediate system or technique, it simply takes too much time and experience to crack the Destiny Code and utilize its teachings. Business leaders in particular aren't interested in the technical details or academic history of BaZi. They don't have time to sit in a classroom - all they want is results!

To this end, I have created a unique format that allows anyone to utilize the BaZi 60 Pillars simply by plotting a chart and turning to the indicated page. I have condensed the original information found in the source texts and updated it with my own experience and findings for the modern world. I've already done all the hard, behind-the-scenes calculations and co-ordination for you. If you can look up information on a reference table and turn the page then you can leverage the full power of the BaZi 60 Pillars.

Creating this rapid delivery version of the 60 Pillars was difficult and time consuming but I know that my efforts will allow people all around the world to use the system for the first time with only a minimum of effort or pre-existing academic understanding. This makes it all worthwhile. The 60 Pillars Life Assessment method *used* to be a system known and understood only by the elite and those in academia - a system passed down in secret from generation to generation. I hope that this series of books finally brings the subject matter to the masses in a digestible, practical way.

I wish you the best of luck in your mission to master the BaZi 60 Pillars! If you wish to delve further into the subject matter after reading, then please do feel free to drop by my FaceBook (www.facebook.com/JoeyYapFB) or attend one of my workshops in the near future. I'll be thrilled to meet you.

Warmest regards,

Joey Yap
May 2013

Author's personal website : www.joeyyap.com

Academy websites : www.masteryacademy.com | www.baziprofiling.com

Joey Yap on Facebook : www.facebook.com/joeyyapFB

INTRODUCTION

INTRODUCTION

In many ways, life seems like a labyrinth which cannot be mapped or fully understood.

Many of us walk through life without a clear understanding of our impact on other people or the way things we do will impact ourselves. This lack of awareness can stunt our potential because we just don't know what we are doing, where we are going, or, if we know where we wish to go, how to get there.

Most commonly, people do not know what their purpose is. This stems from an inability to assess personal talents and abilities. The most successful people - the people who live up to the promise of their Destiny - live to their strengths. When someone has a clear picture of their strengths and weaknesses they would have a better shot at happiness and success. Furthermore, knowing what talents we possess helps us determine what we have the give to the world. The more we can give, the more value we possess in the eyes of those around us.

BaZi is something of a personal map for the labyrinth of life. It will help you to become the best possible version of you!

BaZi Astrology - The Map to Your Life

Your BaZi, or Destiny Code, describes your strengths and weaknesses. It can help you show you the maximum possible personal limits, based on what makes you, you. It dictates how far you can go in life, and what you can possibly achieve with the talent and potential you have been uniquely blessed with.

BaZi allows us to understand our Destiny and ultimately make better choices everyday. We can make a choice either to act upon life, rather than merely allowing life to act upon us.

Studying your BaZi Destiny Chart is similar to peeling an onion. There are many hidden layers of truth that you will uncover as you find out about yourself. By fully understanding your potential, you can both walk the shortest path to achievement and avoid dead ends in life that you are ill equipped to venture down.

BaZi can be used as a tool to:

> **A) Help us understand who we are.**
>
> - Understand our destiny
> - Our character, personality, strengths, weaknesses
> - Talents and abilities

> **B) Map of our life and Destiny.**
>
> - Events and circumstances that could benefit us
> - Events and circumstances that could challenge us
> - What lessons and insights we can gain from our experiences
> - Help us grow
> - Growth and progress leads us to happiness and fulfillment in life

When I speak of Destiny, it is easy to imagine that I mean a concrete series of life events over which you have no control. However, I believe that Destiny is not carved in stone. We all choose to either fulfill our Destiny or to ignore it and fail. Your BaZi chart can help you find your flow, allowing you to fulfill 100% of your potential.

All of us have distinctive talents and capabilities. Recognizing this and knowing exactly what these are can allow you to supercharge your progress and achieve far more than you ever thought possible during your lifetime.

Understanding your BaZi chart, which reveals these distinctive talents and capabilities, is therefore the key to unleashing your innate potential.

So, what are the limitations?

If BaZi is so powerful, why hasn't it helped every person in the world to become wildly successful? While this is certainly possible, one reason is that BaZi Astrology is a complicated affair. I've spent two decades of my life studying and teaching it.

To help make the subject more accessible, I've written five key books on BaZi. Together, they form the **Destiny Code** Series.

This collection of books serves as an introductory platform on BaZi for students, practitioners or teachers to heighten their knowledge and widen their skill.

Another reason that BaZi cannot truthfully guarantee wild riches and success in stone is because we simply cannot control everything that happens to us in life.

We are at the mercy of circumstance and changing fortunes. Going through life is like riding the waves of the ocean; events rush in one after another. Some circumstances, or events are trivial and cause little or no impact to our lives. While others can drastically change the playing field and knock us for six. Think family deaths, injuries and so on.

The good news for BaZi students is that even in the worst circumstances, BaZi allows us to gain control.

With BaZi we can learn what our options are. By understanding our options, we can make better choices - instead of drifting aimlessly down the river, we can choose which fork in the river we wish to travel down. This is the way in which we can all design our own Destiny, no matter what.

The Next Level: BaZi In 2013 And Beyond

It has long been my mission to bring the art and science of BaZi to the masses.

In the course of my BaZi consulting practice over the last seventeen years, I've met with many professionals, leaders of nations and heads of multinationals. I've worked closely with some of Asia's biggest CEOs- people whose lives are interesting and inspirational. These clients lead and inspire thousands of people.

When it comes to BaZi, these busy high achievers are not interested in 'studying the technicalities' - they demand quick methods and fast results. They only want a system which gives them the ability to make split second decisions based on a person's personality and potential (the key information imparted by BaZi, and the information which is of great value in the corporate world!)

Corporate clients simply don't need a FULL "Destiny reading". They are more interested in people development, people management and personality profiling.

They need a tool to help them influence and lead others better.

This realization led me to do further research into the system of BaZi in an attempt to simplify and streamline the system for instant 'personality assessment'. I made it my goal to update BaZi for the modern world.

To this end, I eventually created the "BaZi Profiling System" in order to help people kick start the process of learning about the source of their true perceptions and what they can do to shift their lives for the better without the need to understand the technical aspects of BaZi chart reading.

This lead me to another series of books focusing on personality profiling -which proved very popular among business professionals. For the first time, BaZi became widely accessible to everyone on Earth.

In my many years of BaZi teaching and writing, I have witnessed how the BaZi Profiling System helped thousands of people take control of their lives. Excitingly, the BaZi Personality Profiles are really just the beginning of the BaZi system, however.

What I offer you now is the next level of this profiling system. An advanced user level, if you may. Beyond BaZi Profiling is the traditional **Day Pillar analysis** - a method of reading I use whenever I do a career counseling with job seekers or corporate professionals. This technique is known as - the **60 Pillar Life Analysis** method, known in Chinese as "一柱論命法 *Yi Zhu Lun Ming Fa.*"

This book is intended for both the casual reader and professional practitioner. In this way, it has been written with the same mind set as one of my previous book on the Ten Stars of BaZi - ***The Ten Gods***, which was a success with both of these demographics.

Before we go further, allow me to write a little about the history of BaZi so that you may have a base level of understanding before proceeding to... **A History to BaZi Methodologies.**

The current format of BaZi Astrology study was first introduced in the keystone reference of Zi Ping BaZi, by *XuZi Ping* 徐子平 (907-960), from the North region of the Song Dynasty 北宋. He was a famous author, with far-reaching knowledge in the field of Chinese Astrology that covered the Five Elements, the Ten Gods and various branches of the Chinese Metaphysical studies.

Later *Xu Le Wu* 徐樂吾 (1886 - 1949), a relatively recent scholar of BaZi, greatly contributed to the development of Zi Ping BaZi. His works include the ever-important 窮通寶鑑 *Qiong Tong Bao Jian* and 子平眞訣 *Zi Ping Zhen Jue* that served as an important reference point, especially in the Pictorial Method (an integral part of this book), for all serious BaZi practitioners.

Xu Le Wu's publications of these classics have since become the ideal point of reference in the field - his ideas borrowed, replicated, and reproduced by subsequent practitioners of his time and even up until the present day. Unfortunately, in my humble opinion, many of the modern day authors may have missed some of the important nuances in his original work - and have taken some of his meaning almost too literally.

Zi Ping Cui Yan 子平粹言 was perhaps *Xu Le Wu's* final book, and I believe the author wrote this book with hopes of teaching his students the correct way to use the Pictorial Method and incorporate a deeper understanding of the Five Element Theory.

The ancient texts from this 60 Pillar Life Analysis Method book are mainly derived from the classic reference of *Di Tian Shui* 滴天髓. According to the legend, *Di Tian Shui* is written by *Jing Tu* 京圖, the Yi Jing practitioner of the Song Dynasty. In the early Ming Dynasty, it was further explained and annotated by *Liu Cheng Yi* 劉誠意, who is also known as, the famous scholar - *Liu Bo Wen* 劉伯溫.

The ancient practitioners and teachers of BaZi always referred to the *Di Tian Shui* 滴天髓 as one of the essential references because they believed the information in this book would bring clarity and complete understanding to the learners of this art, if they were able to unlock the meaning within the pages. However, this proved to be quite a challenging task as the classics were written in language that is filled with metaphors and obscure meanings. This has been overlooked by modern day authors who read it literally.

With that said, I applaud the effort of Mr. Hung Hin Cheong, one of the most accomplished students of mine and a successful engineer and corporate manager, in translating ancient passages of the *Di Tian Shui* and making the meaning clear and applicable to today's society. I've taken extracts from his excellent transliteration work and have included them in a section in this book.

Like *Xu Le Wu* 徐樂吾 (1886 - 1949), I realized today that there is a gap between the real science of BaZi and what was being offered or at least perceived in the mass market.

I also understand that another subtle problem facing BaZi today is the popularity of my very own Destiny Code series. I inadvertently created a breed of street-side practitioners who use my Destiny Code series of books. Of course, due to their lack of in-depth understanding of the concepts of the Five Elements and the Yin and Yang, some well-intended educators have merely taught their students the literal meaning of their readings; that is Jia being a big Tree and the Bing as the Sun. Serious practitioners known that the Pictorial Method drills far deeper than that. I hope this new book will help bring this notion to the general public and to the very same street-side practitioners!

At the end of it all, there are several ways to read a BaZi Chart. Each of these systems of analysis has its own benefits. By using these you will be able to look at a BaZi Chart from several different angles.

The Day Pillar Analysis

Using 60 Pillars Analysis in the BaZi system truly takes your BaZi reading to a deeper level. The most important part of the BaZi Chart for this purpose is the Day Pillar which contains the Day Master - an area of the BaZi Chart you will already be intimately familiar with after reading my BaZi Profiling or Destiny Code books.

The Day Pillar is perhaps the most important part of the BaZi Chart when it comes to discovering inner strength. Therefore, a more intricate understanding of the Day Pillar can allow you to greatly appreciate your talents and abilities. This insight can also help you learn how to become a better communicator, a better lover, a better friend, and find success in your life.

While I am a firm believer in positive thinking, I do not subscribe to the belief that we can simply 'psyche' ourselves into finding success or inner peace. I believe positivity is achieved when we are true to our nature. Our innate personality. By appreciating our born talents and capitalizing on them. By truly knowing who we are and becoming a better version of ourselves. I believe we can do this best through enhanced understanding of the BaZi 60 Day Pillars. Learning about the 60 Day Pillars is one way in which we can find our groove and begin climbing the mountain of progress - leading to fulfillment and happiness.

Advancing the Study of BaZi

Some of the more common, traditional ways of reading a BaZi Chart are as follows:

- The Strong Weak Analysis
- Useful God Analysis
- Auxiliary Stars
- Structural Analysis Method
- Five Elements Method
- Ten God Analysis Method
- Pictorial Method
- Na Yin Analysis Method
- Ascending and Descending Qi

My own practice of BaZi has grown over the years. Like any passionate student of BaZi, I first started out seeking revered BaZi masters for guidance and researched the ancient classics to uncover all the so called 'secrets' embedded directly or indirectly from the classics. I hoped to find things that had been lost in translation at the original source. Many 'devotees' (this is what I like to call the extremist researchers) keep digging into the past records and needless to say, most of them become what people would normally describe as the academic ivory towers.

I love the classics and I love pure research but I also like seeing the practical side of Chinese Metaphysics. I want to see it used and applied in the real world. I have found that BaZi has great utility in the business community where RESULTS are what count! (The fact my consulting firm continues to retain top corporate clients using BaZi Profiling in business is probably the best proof that it really does work wonders - if it didn't, we would have been shown the door long ago).

I've worked with the heads of businesses and leaders of nations and I can tell you for a fact - they are not interested in how well I can explain a theory or how well-versed I am in the history of BaZi. They want to know one, simple thing: how can I help them with their business. In other words, they say 'Show Me The Money'.

Over the years, I've come to realize that BaZi could be upgraded and re-packaged for the modern world. It could serve as the beating heart in a new, rapid deployment system for use in business and by people who want accurate results and answers without having to know how the system works or where it came from, necessarily. The 60 Pillars Life Analysis Method that I share with you in this book is an old method that I have brought firmly into the 21st century for today's practical world.

The methods presented here are based on *Xu Le Wu's* original Pictorial description of the Stems. I've taken the liberty to refine them and make the whole thing suitable for the modern audience.

As people continue to learn the BaZi and the tradition grows, there is no doubt in my mind that more of these old and new analysis methods will come forward.

The update and modification I've made also means that I have an additional method to share that is a total revolution to the modern BaZi system. This BaZi reading method is called the new Joey Yap's Pictorial Analysis Method and it is going to completely change the way that people learn BaZi. My goal is to present a comprehensive and wonderful system that is known as the BaZi, in a way that is more understandable and easily digested by the people who have a desire to learn its secrets.

The Pictorial Analysis Method is the next step in my passion project of bringing BaZi to everyone.

The Pictorial Analysis Method

The Pictorial Analysis Method I write of in this book is a shorthand that allows the reader to very quickly assess the 60 Pillars. It is one of the main methods I've used to deduce the meaning and attributes of each of the 60 Pillars. Now this does not mean this is the ONLY format, because we also take into consideration the Five Elements, the Ten Gods, the Twelve Growth and Birth Phases, the Auxiliary Stars and Na Yin components of each pillar. I've incorporated all these into some sort of a picture form for the pillar. Each of the 60 Pillars in this book has an associated picture. This concept relies heavily on the concept of Imagery or images, used as the backbone of Yi Jing (I-Ching), the book of changes, as well as a deep understanding of the Five Elements.

Why have I opted to use this picture-based system?

Learning the BaZi system in depth is a daunting task. This is why I created the BaZi 60 Pillars Analysis Method - in order to help make the system more understandable, palatable, and digestible from several different angles. Instead of reading and memorizing list after list of signs, elements, traits, and ideas, you can learn the BaZi system based off of images that represent the energy behind each of the 60 Pillars.

They do say that a picture paints a thousand words and I am a firm believer in the saying! Many history books as well as classic Chinese literature have used imagery to backup BaZi, just as I do here. In fact, the translations of the specific meanings of the words connected to the BaZi reveal that each sign are called by names that suitably relate to a very specific, defined image. For example:

- Jia 甲 Wood   - Big Tall Tree

- Yi 乙 Wood   - Flower

- Bing 丙 Fire   - Sunlight

- Ding 丁 Fire   - Candle

- Wu 戊 Earth   - Big Rock

- Ji 己 Earth   - Soft Earth

- Geng 庚 Metal   - Large Axe

- Xin 辛 Metal   - Fine Jewelry

- Ren 壬 Water   - Great Ocean

- Gui 癸 Water   - Misty Rain

I have taken these specific and detailed translations and transformed them into a new way of learning, reading, and getting to the heart of the BaZi. The reason my picture-based system works so well is simple - humans are very visual. It is much easier for us to recall an image than it is words, ideas, or phrases. We even think in picture form. When we are working something out in our minds, imagery will form to help us sort out our issues. Pictures and simple imagery help us make sense of our lives. This is why, in my opinion, the Pictorial Analysis Method is so effective. It allows me to directly convey the essence of the BaZi message through imagery. These images are much easier to remember than words.

There are a number of things that should be discussed before the reader begins to use the Pictorial Analysis Method. Mostly, I wish to address the idea that these pictures should NOT be taken completely literally.

Consider the ever popular BaZi 101 remedy: Jia Wood 甲 = A Big Tree. In the ancient classics, for Jia Wood, a 'metaphorical' description is used to describe the Jia. The original author in the ancient classics was trying to portray the Wood of Jia Wood as having similar attributes to a tree.

The tree spoken of here is just a metaphor. One needs to think further, using the imagery of a tree only as a starting point, to grab the real meaning behind the picture. What the author was really saying about Jia Wood is that it embodies the idea of 'growth' (like a tree), it is about production and progress, it is about the starting of a journey or a cycle, etc.

Regrettably, some of my own students who have ventured out to start their own school of BaZi without completing their studies seem to have only taken the 'literal meaning' of the Pictorial Method with them. Some go all out to say that Jia is represented by the Big Tree and if one wants to enhance the element of Jia Wood, he or she is advised to wear green, or plant big trees in their residence. This concept has been taken out of context and is certainly not in line with my teachings or the teachings of this book. I'll say it again: think metaphorically, not literally.

I want to educate students and those that are interested in learning BaZi the correct way to utilize the Pictorial Method - the way I intend to teach in my previous BaZi Module 4 program - and rectify the problem of literal interpretation in BaZi overall.

Further Learning

To complete your BaZi study and practice, you must first know that the Pictorial Method is a very complex subject. A simple class that expands on this topic can go on and on for days. The reason for this is simple: it is important! If you are serious about a solidifying your understanding of BaZi and the 60 Pillars Life Analysis Method in particular, then you need to go the distance. As such, I strongly encourage readers and practitioners to attend my learning programs and classes, to absorb knowledge beyond the pages, and to further their studies in an understandable and accurate manner with a qualified BaZi teacher or better yet, be your own teacher and invest time in studying the classics. Or perhaps, we can even meet in person in my yearly seminars so that I can exchange ideas with you on this wonderful subject called BaZi.

The Pictorial Method is not intended to be used in isolation.

Know that the Pictorial Method only gives a partial answer; it is but one part of the puzzle. The pictures do not necessarily correspond to a good or bad outcome. They are not meant to be taken at literal, face value - use them simply to get a gut feeling about the Pillar in question.

There is a danger that newer students will use the Pictorial Method as something of a crutch, ignoring the importance of the Five Elements in the process.

Remember, the pictures are to help you understand and interpret the meaning of the Pillar, and they do NOT replace the importance of the Five Elements or the Ten Gods in BaZi. BaZi is fundamentally a Five Element study, so bear this in mind. As such, Jia Wood, although a tree, is still fundamentally a WOOD element. It represents growth, progress, production and new beginnings. Though it may be painted as a big tree, it is still very much a WOOD element. Likewise, Bing Fire 丙 may be visualized as the bright and majestic sunlight Fire, but, in fact, this Pillar still belongs to the FIRE element.

Taking the method too literally may lead others to make the wrong assumption as pictorially Jia Wood (Tree) cannot produce the Bing Fire (Sun). This is where the over-simplification of Pictorial Method is evident, for it evokes possible misinterpretation. Jia, being Wood, can always produce Bing as it is Fire. Wood will always produce Fire. The condition, however, needs to be considered. If the Wood is Wet, then producing Fire is difficult. However if the Wood is Dry, the Fire will be produced. You can judge this from looking at the Season or the surrounding elements. The pictures, in this case, help you visualize this.

One also needs to understand that to facilitate their BaZi knowledge, they need to incorporate the knowledge of the Five Elements, the Ten Gods, and the Twelve Growth Phrases, information that I have incorporated in the BaZi 60 Pillars Life Analysis Method series to provide a more comprehensive learning experience to students.

To The Critics

Of course, with a new way of doing things comes criticism. My attempts to expand the ancient teachings with this new system have not gone uncriticized. I accept this and I would even say I expected it! With any breakthrough system, there is going to be a certain amount of criticism. Great masters of the past like *Xu Zi Ping* 徐子平, *Li Xu Zhong* 李虛中, *Xu Le Wu* 徐樂吾, *Ren Tie Qiao* 任鐵樵, *Yuan Shu Shan* 袁樹珊 and *Wei Qian Li* 韋千里 were heavily criticized during their time. Their work is now accepted as ground breaking and progressive. I welcome criticism because I know and I trust that this expansion of the BaZi is going to help this system of Astrology thrive and help people to improve their lives. However, as I tell my students: There are no statues in this world that are erected in honor of a critic.

The BaZi 60 Pillars

What are the BaZi 60 Pillars?

There are 60 possible combinations of the Five Elements and their different polarities which make up the 60 Pillars. Each Pillar has its own Element and in this book you will find that each of these Pillars has its own pictorial representation, too. By seeing these images you will be able to remember the energies that are connected to the different Elements more easily. When you look at the image for each pillar you remember the name and energy behind that pillar. For example, instead of calling it a Wood Rat or a Wood Horse, you will see an image of the energy that equates to Wood Rat or Wood Horse.

Each book in the BaZi 60 Pillars series deals with one of the ten possible Day Masters. As such, one doesn't need to read all the 10 books in the series; only the one associated with his or her Pillar. Each one of the books is largely written with the Day Pillar in mind.

For the Month, the Year, or the Hour Pillar, readers need to make some minor adjustments on their own in order to derive meaning suitable for the reading represented by each Pillar.

These Pillars are made up of the Ten Stems and the Twelve Branches. Each of the Pillars has one Heavenly Stem and one Earthly Branch.

The Heavenly Stem

The Heavenly Stem is known as the prevailing Qi or surface Qi, located at the top of the Pillar. This refers to the external, publicly visible personality and traits of a person. Here we learn about the personality, traits, and outlook that an individual shows to the world. It is the characteristic, personality or outlook that your friends, family, acquaintances know.

There are ten Heavenly Stems in total; they are made up of the Yin and Yang polarities of the Five Elements:

- Jia 甲 (Yang) Wood
- Yi 乙 (Yin) Wood
- Bing 丙 (Yang) Fire
- Ding 丁 (Yin) Fire
- Wu 戊 (Yang) Earth
- Ji 己 (Yin) Earth
- Geng 庚 (Yang) Metal
- Xin 辛 (Yin) Metal
- Ren 壬 (Yang) Water
- Gui 癸 (Yin) Water

Earthly Branch

The Earthly Branch is the bottom of the Pillar. Think of the hidden roots of a tree. It is the foundation - where your Pillar rests - and therefore, it represents the foundation of who you are.

The Earthly Branch carries the Qi and is considered a stronger influence on an individual's life than the Heavenly Stem is, albeit one which is hidden to others. When we assess the Earthly Branch, we can get a glimpse into the real, secret and hidden attitudes and nature of a person.

The Earthly Branch plays an important role in BaZi analysis as it not only carry the force of time but also represent the seasons and tells us about the strengths of the elements in the Chart.

The Palaces

In the BaZi system the Earthly Branches are made up of Four Pillars. Each of the Pillars signifies a different aspect of your life. The Day Pillar is the most significant because it is made up of both the Heavenly Stem and the Earthly Branch and it is determined by your date of birth, also known as your Day Master.

The Four Pillars

- Hour
- Day
- Month
- Year

時 Hour	日 Day	月 Month	年 Year	
				天干 Heavenly Stems
				地支 Earthly Branches
				十藏 Hidden Stems

The Hour Pillar

This is the Pillar that is connected to your ambitions, hopes and dreams. This is the Pillar of inspiration and your inner personality. The Hour Pillar can also tell us about life in old age as well as relationships with children and subordinates.

Hour Pillar Breakdown	
Conventional View	- Heavenly Stem and Earthly Branch : Children
Life Path	- Heavenly Stem and Earthly Branch : Old Age
Family Relation	- Heavenly Stem: Son - Earthly Branch: Daughter
Psychological Makeup	- Earthly Branch: Entertainment and treatment of subordinates
Psychological View	- Heavenly Stem: Passion - Earthly Branch: Desire

XIN

時 Hour	日 Day	月 Month	年 Year	
				Heavenly Stems
				Earthly Branches
				Hidden Stems

The Day Pillar

This is the Pillar that is determined by the Day Master. It is connected to your inner spirit and your soul. This reveals the way that you communicate with others and the world around you. It also describes physical health. Finally, the Day Pillar is representative of your connection with your spouse.

XIN

Day Pillar Breakdown	
Conventional View	- Heavenly Stem: Self - Earthly Branch: Spouse
Life Path	- Heavenly Stem and Earthly Branch : Mid Age
Family Relation	- Heavenly Stem: Self - Earthly Branch: Spouse
Psychological Makeup	- Heavenly Stem: Inner Spirit - Earthly Branch: Affinity
Psychological View	- Heavenly Stem: Personal view of life - Earthly Branch: Physical body

時 Hour	日 Day	月 Month	年 Year	
				天干 Heavenly Stems
				地支 Earthly Branches
				藏干 Hidden Stems

The Month Pillar

This Pillar is connected to your ambitions. It will also offer insight on your character and your upbringing. It is also connected to the way you handle responsibility and your self control. It can also show you the effect your parents have had and continue to have upon your life. Finally, this Pillar governs your likely career success and/or your business achievements.

Month Pillar Breakdown	
Conventional View	- Heavenly Stem and Earthly Branch: Parents
Life Path	- Heavenly Stem and Earthly Branch: Youth
Family Relation	- Heavenly Stem: Father - Earthly Branch: Mother
Psychological Makeup	- Earthly Branch: Responsibility and self control
Psychological View	- Heavenly Stem: Ambition - Earthly Branch: Character and upbringing

The Year Pillar

This is the Pillar that is connected to your overall gratitude for life. It can describe your morals and ethical integrity. It also describes the way you handle the important matters in your life. The Year Pillar is the cornerstone of your approach to family. It is connected to your relationships with your grandparents and your ancestors. In a modern context, The Year Pillar also represents one's social status and chosen circle of friends.

Year Pillar Breakdown	
Conventional View	- Heavenly Stem and Earthly Branch: Grandparents
Life Path	- Heavenly Stem and Earthly Branch: Childhood
Family Relation	- Heavenly Stem: Ancestor Home - Earthly Branch: Ancestor Tomb
Psychological Makeup	- Earthly Branch: Way of handling matters
Psychological View	- Heavenly Stem: Health - Earthly Branch: Gratitude, morals, and family

時 Hour	日 Day	月 Month	年 Year
				Heavenly Stems
				Earthly Branches
				Hidden Stems

XIN

The Hour Pillar and the Day Pillar are both connected to the internal side of your personality. These two Pillars represent your inner self that you keep hidden from others. Interestingly, these are the parts of yourself that you might not even be aware of. See if what you read rings true!

The Applications

As the BaZi 60 Pillars series is written in the context of the Day Pillar, some adjustments are needed in the event where the Month, Year or the Hour Pillar is read.

Before you begin your learning, you need to find out your own Day Pillar, by plotting out your personal BaZi chart (Go to **www.joeyyap.com/bzchart**). Look at the Day Pillar and find the correct book in the series that matches it. For instance, if your Day Pillar is Gui Wei 癸未, you will need to study the Gui 癸 (Yin Water) Pillar book. Similarly, look for the Ding 丁 (Yin Fire) Pillar book if Ding Hai 丁亥 is your Day Pillar.

時 Hour	日 Day	月 Month	年 Year	
	癸 Gui Yin Water			天干 Heavenly Stems
	未 Wei Goat Yin Earth			地支 Earthly Branches
	乙 Yi - Wood 食 EG / 己 Ji - Earth 殺 7K / 丁 Ding - Fire 才 IW			藏干 Hidden Stems

The BaZi Chart above indicates that the Day Pillar is Gui Wei 癸未. Therefore, refer to the Gui 癸 (Yin Water) Pillar book to read the Pillar's analysis.

時 Hour	日 Day	月 Month	年 Year	
	丁 Ding Yin Fire (DM)			Heavenly Stems 天干
	亥 Hai Pig Yin Water (Conceived 胎)			Earthly Branches 地支
	壬 Ren + Water 官 DO / 甲 Jia + Wood 卯 DR			Hidden Stems 藏干

XIN 辛

The BaZi Chart above indicates that the Day Pillar is Ding Hai 丁亥. Therefore, refer to the Ding 丁 (Yin Fire) Pillar book to read the Pillar's analysis.

In this method, the Day Pillar is read as the primary Pillar of your life. It is placed up in front in the foreground with the most power, control, and influence in your life.

The remaining three Pillars; the Year Pillar, the Month Pillar, and the Hour Pillar, are all in the background. They will affect, support, and change the energy of the Day Pillar. Learning to understand the interaction between the foreground and the background will tremendously enhance the effectiveness of your readings.

The Format of this Book

There are five sections in each individual Pillar. This breakdown of information allows for systematic learning.

The subject of Chinese Metaphysics was founded on the principles of Yi Jing, based on the concept of Qi 氣 (Five Elements), Numerology 數 (methods, methodology, formulae), and Images 像 (The essence of the Pictorial Method). While the Pictorial Method references the third technique (Images), it shouldn't be applied or studied in a manner that is mutually exclusive of the other two.

Therefore these books are written to include these two aspects. At the same time, however, there's a dilemma that if I make the book too technical, students would have a hard time comprehending the information due to the lack of groundwork.

To make the information more accessible, I divided the book into five sections for each Pillar. The first section is written in layman style, with very basic character analysis and personality assessment. The second section and beyond drill in on the technical analysis and reveals some of the working behind the 60 Pillars, hopefully to pique your interest in furthering your study by researching on the more notable ancient classics such as *Qiong Tong Bao Jian* 窮通寶鑒, *Zi Ping Zhen Quan* 子平眞詮, *Di Tian Sui* 滴天髓, *Zi Ping Zhen Jue* 子平眞訣, *Zi Ping Jing Cui* 子平精粹.

Before Each Chapter

Several images that embody the many possible representations of the Pillar are presented in this section. This serves as a pictorial guide to help you better visualize each Pillar as you study.

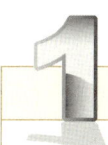

First Section
General descriptions of the Stems
(For all the Stems in a Pillar).

This part gives an overview of each Stem, and provides you with a general impression before you delve deeper into the following sections.

Second Section
Classic Extraction from Di Tian Shui 滴天髓

This section is extracted from the works by Mr. Hung Hin Cheong, who spent countless hours translating the ancient texts of Di Tian Sui. The classical texts of Di Tian Sui provide a solid platform for any learner of BaZi of any experience level to begin and advance their knowledge in the field. The book of Di Tian Sui can be divided into two chapters: Tong Shen Lun 通神論' (The Theosophy) and Liu Qin Lun 六親論 (The Six Relations).

As a side note, in my opinion any serious students of BaZi should try to study and unlock the information in the Di Tian Sui on their own or with a qualified teacher. It is after all, the book of foundation in BaZi study.

Third Section
General Observation of the Pillar

Matters of marriage, career, wealth and family are expanded upon in this section. This section is mercifully written in a simple way, free from jargon and technical lingo. You can also look at the section on Famous Personalities where notable people with similar Day Pillar are listed. These famous case studies help better illustrate the information given.

Fourth Section
Technical Analysis

This section contains some technical aspects pertaining to this BaZi Pillar. It is necessary to have some prior knowledge on BaZi to fully grasp the content in this section.

Fifth Section
The 60 Pillars Unique Combination

Assess the likely outcome of different Pillars combinations; good or bad. You can also learn the specific structure name and advance your skills by understanding the analysis behind each combination.

DO THIS FIRST

Print your BaZi Chart to facilitate your learning process as you use this book.

To plot your BaZi Chart :

www.masteryacademy.com/regbook

Here is your unique code to access the BaZi Calculator:

QLM0627

The following steps will guide you to plot your BaZi Chart with ease.

Step 1 : Upon access to the site, key in the required information - Name, Gender, Hour, Day, Month and Year of Birth - as per instruction

Step 2 : Your BaZi Chart will be generated accordingly. (A sample is illustrated below.)

Step 3 : Print your BaZi Chart.

Step 4 : Begin CHAPTER 1.

Sample: This is how your BaZi Chart will look like

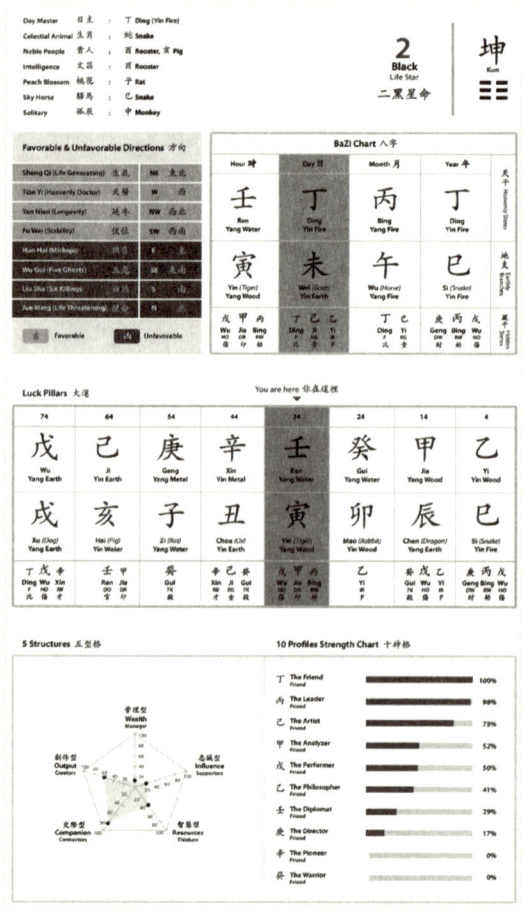

Xin 辛 (Yin Metal)

Xin 辛 Metal individuals are elegant, classy and sophisticated. The associated imagery is that of valuable jewellery or a sparkling diamond. They are elegant, fabulous, special, and unique. When a composed Xin Metal person enters the room, people find it hard to ignore their presence. They enjoy being exposed to new ideas and experiences. They are open minded and ready to live life to the max!

Often witty and charming, others may find them entertaining and nothing makes the Xin Metal happier than being the centre of attention. They can compromise given good reason, not completely stubborn or selfish. They are driven to better themselves so they can enjoy ever finer things.

Xin Metal individuals have a taste for luxury and this can translate into greed and a superficial personality. They may appear thick skinned but inside, they can be soft and easily hurt or offended. They talk a good game but might not truly be able to deliver on promises or back up their confidence with results. They are prone to being moody if things don't go their way, or if they are bored. Nobody is happy when they are bored, but the great difficulty is that Xin Metal individuals are bored very easily. They are vain and can also be somewhat self-centred. Other people often pander to Xin Metal individuals's every whim, feeding this negative trait. Without the appreciation of others, they can lack a healthy sense of self-worth.

DI TIAN SUI 滴天髓

The Classic Text

Introduction

The information presented in this book comes from the original source, the famous classical text on BaZi called **Di Tian Sui** 滴天髓.

Di Tian Sui 滴天髓 can be credited as one of the important works of Liu Bo Wen 劉伯溫, a renowned military strategist, statesman and metaphysics scholar in the late Yuan and early Ming period of the 14th century. Liu Bo Wen was highly regarded for his contributions in the study of astronomy, Feng Shui as well as philosophy.

Liu Bo Wen was also a poet, and when he composed the original Di Tian Sui texts, he wrote it as a poem. Thus, the language used was so cryptic that scholars over the decades continue to find it a challenge to decipher the poem's true meaning.

In the following pages, you will find the original text on Xin Metal as written by Liu Bo Wen and its interpretation and transliteration extracted from Mr Hung Hin Cheong. Mr Hung has also contributed his commentary on the original texts in this book.

Xin Metal According to Di Tian Sui 滴天髓

Original Text by Liu Bo Wen

辛金軟弱，溫潤而清，
畏土之疊，樂水之盈，
能扶社稷，能救生靈，
熱則喜母，寒則喜丁。

Interpretation by Hung Hin Cheong

Soft and weak, **Xin Metal** is elegant and lucid. Fears heavy earth, but desires abundant water. Able to support society, and save life and spirit. Likes its mother when hot, likes ding when cold.

Commentary by Hung Hin Cheong:

The lucid and elegant attributes of Xin (辛) Metal embody the gentle harmonious Qi of the 3 Autumn months.

Excessive Wu (戊) Earth will dry up the Water and bury the Metal. Abundant Ren (壬) Water will moisten the Earth to yield up the Metal within.

Xin is husband to Jia (甲), and Bing (丙) is husband to Xin. Bing is able to burn Jia Wood, but Xin combines with Bing transforming to Water, thereby turning a regulatory force into a resource. Hence the phrase "support society (Bing, the husband) and save the life and spirit (Jia, the wife)".

If born in Summer with excessive Fire, the presence of Ji (己) Earth will dim the Fire and produce Metal.

If born in Winter with a deluge of Water, the presence of Ding (丁) Fire will warm up the Water and nurture Metal.

Hence the word "likes".

辛丑

Xin Chou

| 辛丑 | 辛卯 | 辛巳 | 辛未 | 辛酉 | 辛亥 |
| Xin Chou | Xin Mao | Xin Si | Xin Wei | Xin You | Xin Hai |

Getting to Know
Xin Chou 辛丑 (Metal Ox)

Positive Imagery

Negative Imagery

辛丑
Metal Ox

Getting to Know
Xin Chou 辛丑 (Metal Ox)

General Observations:

The image representation of the Xin Chou is raw metal coming from the ground. This unpolished element in its original form reflects the Xin Chou personality that is pure and solid.

Those born in the Xin Chou Pillar are idealistic, intuitive and self-confident. As natural born leaders, they are likely to live an influential life. They are considered very good looking, which along with their charming personality, gives them a competitive edge in most circumstances. Generally, the Xin Chou are considered by others as optimistic, intelligent, humanitarian and simply remarkable.

The Xin Chou are inherently wise and perceptive. Their wisdom guides them in making accurate decisions while their perception causes them to be receptive to the lessons that life is trying to teach them. For this reason, they are considered great "life learners". In addition, they also have a heightened appreciation for art and other creative pursuits.

They are also swift thinkers. Their quick thinking helps them to wriggle out of unpleasant situations and avoid trouble.

Xin Chou individuals desire to maintain harmony in their lives. They are spiritually inclined and will usually put forth great effort to maintain a sense of purity and innocence.

Resources will be abundantly available for the Xin Chou all the days of their life. This will be especially true if they learn the discipline of hard work. In fact, mastering the discipline of hard work, will cause them to find success everywhere they turn. They will rarely find themselves lacking in material goods and will instead always be surrounded by food, clothing and all of the good things in life. Furthermore, they are likely to inherit property from their ancestors.

As for Xin Chou Pillar females, they will have access to all of the best things in life and will bring prosperity to their family. They are also likely to have difficulty having children and can expect to have a relativity small family of their own.

Xin Chou individuals are highly loyal to those in their life. They will make real sacrifices for the people that they care about and will do whatever it takes to make those around them happy and comfortable.

Although they are loyal, they must be careful not to devote themselves to situations that are mentally and emotionally unhealthy for them. It can lead to negative thinking and self-degradation.

Because Xin Chou individuals are meticulous about plans and details, they may become overcritical of themselves if things do not work out as planned. They must learn to avoid impatience, restlessness, and self-criticism.

Metal
Ox

Key Character Traits of the Xin Chou 辛丑: Overall

- Sociable
- Intuitive
- Creative
- Practical
- Self-Confident
- Impatient
- Hardworking

Work Life

Xin
Chou

Professional Self

There are a wide range of career opportunities for those born under this Pillar due to their intelligence and creativity. Xin Chou individuals retain a special combination of optimism and leadership which can make them highly successful on their career path. A career that provides variety in their daily routine will make them happiest. They need to search for a job that does not require them to be submissive or in a level where they do not have the freedom to be more independent in their roles.

Their desire to share their lessons and experiences enable them to work well with others. Working well with others gives them the best opportunities for careers that involve diplomacy and counselling. On the other hand, their flair for the dramatic can serve them well in career pursuits involving creativity.

Their inherent diligence motivates them to put their all into whatever project they take up. Because they are perfectionists, they expect things to always go as planned. If a project does not turnout as planned, they will become impatient, and critical.

Their altruistic nature provides them with the skills to work best for charities or organisations with movements and causes they believe in.

Career Options

The best careers for the Xin Chou are careers that utilize their natural ingenious skills. Music, acting, directing, and other artistic pursuits will appeal to their creative fundamental nature.

In addition to their creative skills, they are also visionaries. They could apply their far-sightedness in concepts and ideas to careers in advertising, publishing or other media forms.

Metal Ox

Their desire to share knowledge would make them excellent teachers or writers, while their practical side may lead them into careers as counsellors, or advisors.

An inherent down-to-earth approach may lead them into therapeutic and healing professions.

Their astuteness and leadership skills suggest they may be appropriate for some career in diplomacy. They would also be successful in the world of business, commerce and engineering because of their ambition, practicality and dedication.

Metal
Ox

Key Character Traits of the Xin Chou 辛丑: Work life

Positive

- Creative
- Artistic
- Positive Mindset
- Dedicated
- Natural Leader
- Ambitious
- Practical

Negative

- Overly Critical
- Emotionally Detached
- Arrogant
- Rigid
- Bossy
- Easily Bored
- Unfocused
- Judgmental

Love and Relationships

Xin
Chou

Love

Xin Chou individuals are highly expressive, charming and romantic. They tend to give all of themselves in relationships and because of this, potential suitors will vie for their affection.

Ideally, they are drawn to others who have strong and dramatic personalities. However, what they want and what they need do not always match. What they really need is someone responsible who can provide them with an anchor and stability.

They are not lazy or complacent in their marriages. Instead, they will do whatever it takes to help out their partner and ensure that the relationship runs smoothly. For this reason, their relationships are highly beneficial.

Marriage will also increase the Xin Chou's social status. Generally, Xin Chou women will benefit from marriage more than Xin Chou men. They both, however, will experience an increase in social status as a result of marriage.

Although they do take their relationships seriously, they need to be careful not to become overly committed in their relationships. If their partners are not appreciative of their commitment, the Xin Chou will lose their inner balance. Losing their balance in a relationship will cause them to become inflexible and difficult.

Acquaintances

All friendships are meaningful to Xin Chou individuals. Their outgoing personality, along with their love of meeting new people, will ensure the Xin Chou a life full of friendship.

Their amiable personality draws people to them, which is why the Xin Chou are often involved in many social settings and engagements, always surrounded by friends old and new.

They are viewed as loyal, caring, and dedicated by their friends and when it comes to their inner circle, they are supportive and protective.

There is not much that will prevent them from going above and beyond for those truly closest to them. Their generosity will lead them to give more than is necessary to their loved ones. Benevolence and compassion are the ultimate goals in all of their friendships.

Metal Ox

Family

The Xin Chou are highly supportive of their family and are committed to doing all that they can for them.
Marriage is highly beneficial for them. Once the Xin Chou and their partner pull together, they are able to make a real impact in their family.

Marriage for the female is rewarding and satisfying. She will bring good luck, wealth and prosperity to her family.

Xin Chou individuals also have hard luck when it comes to children. Either they have a tough time conceiving them or are unable to have them at all. They may also become frustrated and jealous of others with children if this happens.

While the Xin Chou strive for harmony, they can become frustrated when things do not go according to plan. It may cause them to become rigid and negative. They must also avoid becoming immersed in jealously.

Key Character Traits of the Xin Chou 辛丑: Love & Relationships

- Dedicated and Loyal
- Women will benefit more from marriage
- Difficulty Conceiving
- Attracted to Dramatic Personalities
- Potential for losing themselves in relationships
- Compassionate
- Generous to Loved Ones

Metal
Ox

Famous Personalities

Lee Myung Bak - The 10th President of South Korea. He was also the CEO of Hyundai Engineering and Construction, and the mayor of Seoul.

David Cameron - Prime Minister of the United Kingdom. He became the youngest British Prime Minister at aged forty-three when he assumed office on May 11, 2010.

Source: Wikipedia (June 2013)

Technical Analysis

Xin
Chou

BaZi Day Pillar Analytics 日柱分析

時 Hour	日 Day	月 Month	年 Year	
	辛 Xin Yin Metal (日元 DM)			天干 Heavenly Stems
	丑 Chou Ox Yin Earth (養 Nourishing)			地支 Earthly Branches
	辛 Xin - Metal 比 F　己 Ji - Earth 卩 IR　癸 Gui - Water 食 EG			藏干 Hidden Stems

Metal Ox

Description

This Xin Metal sits on the Resource 印星, Friend 比星 and Eating God 食神星 Stars, and they are rooted at the hidden Stem. This configuration suggests that these individuals will have a natural elegance and nobility. Women of this Pillar will tend to be very beautiful, slender and graceful. They will have a deep love for their family and will work hard to take care of them.

People born under the Xin Chou Pillar will be driven to create a unique identity. They will want to stand out from the crowd and to feel that they are different and special. They have a flair for the dramatic and will tend to take centre stage. For all this, however, they often need to work to overcome their tendency to succumb to peer pressure.

Xin Chou individuals are incredibly creative and deeply imaginative. This is the effect of the hidden Eating God

Star. They are adaptable and resourceful with enough drive and resilience to make things happen and turn their visions into concrete reality. They are very ambitious and decisive with a good business sense and they often aspire to management positions. Their desire to create order often means that they perform well in these roles and leadership will also allow them to express their ideas without restriction.

Though the Xin Chou will put across an image of being very confident they may be far more sensitive and vulnerable than they like people to see. This can be attributed to the Indirect Resource Star偏印星that this Pillar sits on. They often find it very hard to express their deeper emotions even to those closest to them. They can be given to extremes and their lives are often rollercoasters of emotion. It may be advisable for them to take time away from their lives in order rest and rediscover their emotional equilibrium.

The Xin Chou individual is very humanitarian. They are faithful and honest with a great attachment to home and family. Their emotional nature leads them to crave stability and they will work hard to create a secure and harmonious home.

Technical Observations

The Xin Chou is likely to be wealthy and prosperous in life, should their Pillar be supported by the positive presence of Wu 戊, Geng 庚, Yin 寅 (Tiger), Xu 戌 (Dog), Chen 辰 (Dragon) and Zi 子 (Rat). If this Pillar is met with a Clash 冲, Punishment 刑 and Destruction 破, however, the outcome is often far less positive, and these individuals may struggle to achieve their financial or relationship goals as it is likely that many of their greatest qualities will not be able to manifest.

The Xin Chou 辛丑 who meets with an additional Friend Star 比肩星 in the BaZi Chart are likely to be more loyal than those who meet with the Rob Wealth Star 劫財星.

People under this configuration who were born in the Spring or Summer seasons will benefit from Noble help and will find that they are helped towards success by friends, family and colleagues. People who are born in the Autumn or Winter seasons, however, are likely to have to work hard to achieve success based on their own efforts.

Individuals born during the daylight hours (5AM - 5PM) will find that they need to break out of their comfort zone and really work proactively if they wish to achieve success. A Xin Chou born during the nighttime (5PM - 5AM) is likely to have variable fortunes throughout the first half of their life. If the individual was born in the month of the Shen 申 (Monkey), they may find that they struggle to achieve and they will not be able to acquire wealth until later in life due to the presence of the Rob Wealth Star in the Month Branch.

Unique 60 Pillar Combinations

This section covers the relationships between the individual pillar under this elemental polarity and several other pillars found in the 60 Jia Zi cycle.

Xin
Chou

Heaven Combine Earth Punish 天合地刑
Xin Chou 辛丑 (Metal Ox) + Bing Xu 丙戌 (Fire Dog)

This Pillar combines with the Heavenly Stem, but forms a Punishment with the Earthly Branch. As the Heavenly Stem forms a part of the combination a positive outlook and apparent happiness is indicated, but as the Earthly Branch forms a Punishment it brings with it tension, emotional pain, and stress. The interpretation here is that the individual will be hiding their true feelings behind a performance of well-being.

An individual may encounter this Heaven Combine Earth Punish in their BaZi Natal Chart in the Year, Month, Hour, Luck Pillars, or Annual Pillar.

If this Heaven Combine Earth Punish appears in the Year Pillar, it is likely that the individual will appear to have a favourable relationship with their grandparents, but they will be hiding feelings of tension and unhappiness behind a positive façade.

If this configuration is seen in the Month Pillar, the individual may play the part of the devoted son or daughter but their true feelings are likely to be far more complex. In reality the relationship will quite strained and they are unlikely to be able to communicate effectively. A position here could also indicate that the individual is unhappy in their career. It is likely that the individual will be very stressed at work and they will fear that they are unable to trust their colleagues. Their days will be dominated by anxiety over office politics, however much of their anxiety will be unfounded. They will not be able to overcome their emotions until they learn to relax.

In the Hour Pillar, this configuration suggests that the individual will need to learn not to make empty promises. They are likely to want nothing more than to please others and so they accept every task. They need to understand that they cause greater disappointment in the long term by failing to fulfil their commitments than they will do if they simply decline a request in the first instance.

When this configuration is discovered in the Luck Pillar, it is an indication that the individual will not be able to recognise their own worth. They will be successful and admired but they will not feel worthy of their good fortune. If they do not work to repair their self-esteem they will start to impair their own progress.

If this configuration is found in the Annual Pillars, the individual may find that the year will contain many promising deals that fall apart at the last minute. It is likely that tension in the work place and the apparent distrust of colleagues will cause them to panic and start making unnecessary changes and it is these changes that are likely to be the direct cause of the Xin Chou's plans going astray. They are advised to remain calm and to recognise that fear is the true enemy here.

Heaven Combine Earth Harm 天合地害
Xin Chou 辛丑 (Metal Ox) + Bing Wu 丙午 (Fire Horse)

This Heaven Combine Earth Harm Pillar combines with the Heavenly Stem, but forms a Harm 害 with the Earthly Branch. The outlook indicated by the Heavenly Stem would appear to be very positive, but the individual will be hiding feelings of uncertainty and distrust inflicted by the Harm formation.

An individual may encounter this Heaven Combine Earth Harm Pillar if it appears in their Natal Chart in either the Year, Month, or Hour, the Luck Pillars, or the Annual Pillar.

In the Natal Chart, if the Heaven Combine Earth Harm configuration is seen in the Year Pillar it indicates that the individual will be confused and unsure about their relationship with their grandparents. There may appear to be a positive bond on the surface but the individual will not have a great deal of faith in it. Alternatively the individual may lack confidence in their friendships.

If this configuration is visible in the Month Pillar, the individual is likely to be harbouring secret doubts about their relationships with the authority figures in their lives. They may have concerns about their bond with their parents and worry that their parents are keeping things from them. Alternatively they may fear that their managers or supervisors at work will abuse their loyalty and take advantage of their hard work.

In the Hour Pillar, this configuration suggests that the individual will worry about the loyalty of their children. It is possible that their children will choose to confide in their grandparents rather than in their Xin Chou parent and that this will be interpreted as a betrayal. Alternatively the individual may have an uneasy relationship with their customers, clients and suppliers.

If this configuration is apparent in the Luck Pillar, it suggests that the individual will be unable to find peace in their success and that they will feel abused and victimised. It is likely that the individual will have achieved a great deal but far from feeling pride in their accomplishments they instead feel jaded and tired. It is possible that their apparent good fortune has come with an unexpected price to pay.

In the Annual Pillar, this configuration indicates a year of great promise that nevertheless ends in disappointment. The individual will need to look inside themselves for the true source for their feelings. It is likely that they will have achieved all they had set out to and all that could have been expected of them but they have allowed jealousy to distort their judgement and change their perception. They need to remember not to compare themselves with others and to be content with themselves.

Heaven Friend Earth Clash 天比地冲
Xin Chou 辛丑 (Metal Ox) + Xin Wei 辛未 (Metal Goat)

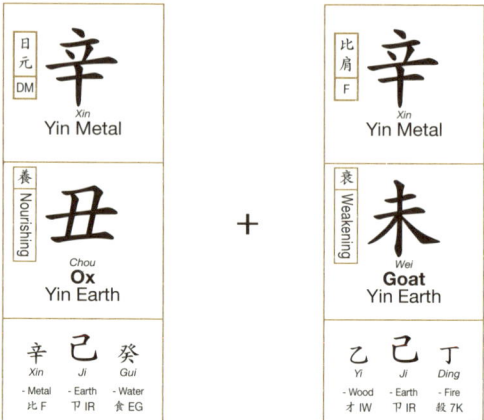

This Pillar shares the same Heavenly Stem but creates a Clash 冲 formation at the Earthly Branch. This Pillar suggests that what may begin with agreements may see its end in disagreements and discord.

It is likely that an individual with this configuration in their Chart will find that their achievements fall far short of the energy and activity that they put into their lives. They will almost certainly be very busy and will have a packed schedule for the most part but their efforts may prove to be empty and they will accomplish very little material success. Outcomes are likely to differ from expectations and the individual will be left unsettled and disappointed but there may yet be a positive in all this. The Heavenly Stem holds the key, and if it proves to be favourable, even an apparently negative turn of events will prove to have a beneficial effect in the long term.

An individual may encounter the Heaven Friend Earth Clash if it appears in their BaZi Natal Chart in either the Year, Month, or Hour, the Luck Pillars, or the Annual Pillar.

If the Heaven Friend Earth Clash appears in the Year Pillar of the Natal Chart, these events and emotions will have an impact on the individual's relationships with their grandparents and friends. Some unexpected news or a change in circumstances may push these relationships off balance.

If this configuration is found in the Month Pillar, the individual may find that their relationship with their parents is altered in some way that they could not have foreseen. Alternatively they may find that their career plans are suddenly derailed. Though these events may be concerning at the time if the Heavenly Stem is favourable, these changes may ultimately prove to have a very positive effect.

In the Hour Pillar, this configuration may have a bearing on the individual's relationship with their children, on their connection to their employees and even their ideas and contributions to society. It's possible that a sudden change in perspective or new thoughts about their direction may cause the individual to make changes in their life that will have an impact on their children and on their working relationships.

If this configuration is discovered in the Luck Pillar, it indicates a period of steady change. This will be a time of growth and progression. The process may be difficult and even painful, but ultimately it will prove to be a positive. The lessons the individual learns during this time will stand them in good stead to achieve their goals; they just need to be patient.

In the Annual Pillar, this configuration suggests that the year will be dominated by surprises and unexpected twists and turns. The individual is likely to face many personal struggles as their plans and expectations are thrown off course and their emotions and perspectives are shaken. They are likely to learn a tremendous amount about themselves during the year and will emerge enriched by new insight.

Heaven and Earth Clash 天沖地沖
Xin Chou 辛丑 (Metal Ox) + Ding Wei 丁未 (Fire Goat)

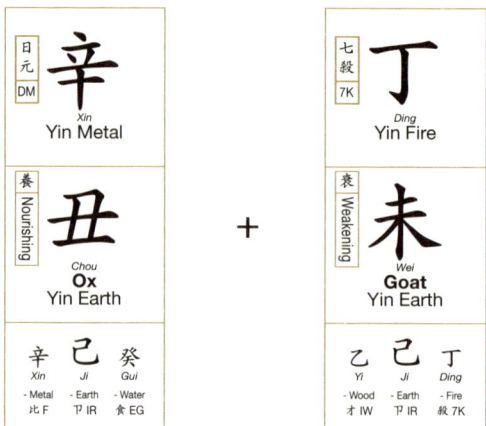

This Heaven and Earth Clash Pillar is a configuration in which the Day Pillar clashed by the Ding Wei 丁未 Pillar. This is known as the Fan Yin 反吟 formation and it is an unlucky formation because it will act to diminish any of the good qualities of an individual's Day Pillar. This formation will impair the individuals chances of achieving success based on their own merits and may also have the effect of placing more barriers in their way. It is likely that the individual will find that their path to success is littered with obstacles that they are ill-equipped to overcome.

Anyone connected to the Xin Chou with this Pillar in their Chart runs the risk of having a negative impact on their career. They may have on the Xin Chou individual's best interests at heart but they may nevertheless be the source of poor advice or they may simply be a distraction.

Seen in the Natal Chart, this configuration indicates a lack of affinity with the individual or individuals represented by the specific Pillar in which it appears.

When this configuration is found in the Year Pillar, the individual is likely to experience a lack of affinity with their grandparents and friends. It could be that the individual finds that they work a lot of hours and that by the time they have dispensed with their familial responsibilities they have no time left for these people.

In the Month Pillar, this configuration suggests the individual will have little affinity with their parents. They will struggle to connect with their parents on an intellectual or emotional level and they may find that their perspectives are too disparate to be reconciled. Alternatively the individual may feel that they are unable to win the recognition of their managers and supervisors or that they are ill suited to perform in cooperative endeavours.

If this configuration is present in the Hour Pillar, it can mean that the individual feels a lack of affinity with their children. It could be that they have step children and that they are unable to build a positive relationship with them. Alternatively they may find that they can't relate to their customers or clients and that this is affecting their ability to deliver a good service. Finally, a position in the Hour could suggest that the individual feels that they have completely lost step with the world and that they don't know how to make a contribution to society.

In the Luck Pillar, this configuration is an indication of a period of painful change, stress and obstacles. The individual may feel that nothing is working in their favour and this will understandably cause them some upset, they are advised to find comfort and solace in trusted friends.

If this configuration occurs in the Annual Pillar, it is recommended that the individual keep a low profile for the year. They should avoid making any major decisions or significant changes where possible. It would also be wise for them to refrain from making any serious financial investments. Any plans should be postponed until the next year as the individual is unlikely to enjoy the best of luck at this time.

Heaven Counter Earth Clash 天剋地沖
Xin Chou 辛丑 (Metal Ox) + Yi Wei 乙未 (Wood Goat)

This Heaven Counter Earth Clash Pillar is a configuration in which the Day Pillar is going against the Yi Wei乙未. It is important to note that this configuration and the Heaven and Earth Clash formations are different. In this situation, the individual of this Pillar is placed in a position of control. They will have passion and a strong desire to win. They are likely to be dominant characters with an entrepreneurial spirit who have the potential to achieve great success but they must be careful not to be impatient or over hasty in their decision making.

An individual may encounter this Heaven Counter Earth Clash Pillar if it appears in their Natal Chart in either the Year, Month, or Hour Pillar, as well as the Luck Pillars, or the Annual Pillar.

When this configuration is visible in the Year Pillar, it suggests that the individual will benefit from the assistance of high-profile friends. Should they choose to strike out alone and begin their own business these people will be able to assist them with advice, contacts, product promotion and even the possibility of investment.

It this configuration is found in the Month Pillar, it suggests that the individual will be money minded with a flair for business and a passion for turning a profit. They may however be inclined to becoming avaricious and may need to guard against allowing greed to motivate them.

In the Hour Pillar, this configuration suggests that the individual may take dedication and hard work to an extreme and that they will lose sight of their other responsibilities. These individuals may need to be reminded that their families need more than just material support and that happiness is not built on career success alone.

Metal Ox

When seen in the Luck Pillar, this configuration suggests that the individual will be ambitious and driven. They will work hard to advance in their careers and to increase their material wealth. The individual is advised to make the most of this time as they are likely to be blessed with luck in their financial investments. They should aim to keep a level head however and think carefully about their decisions.

If this configuration is seen in the Annual Pillar, the individual is likely to encounter a myriad opportunities to advance and to invest. They may begin a new venture or become involved in new working partnerships. This is likely to be a very positive year in terms of financial growth and career progression. In terms of health and family, however, the year is likely to be the cause of some stress and strain. Although it would be wise to work hard and take advantage of their success, the individual is also advised to take just a little time for their personal lives and their physical well-being.

Heaven and Earth Unity 天同地比
Xin Chou 辛丑 (Metal Ox) + Xin Chou 辛丑 (Metal Ox)

This configuration is traditionally known as the Fu Yin 伏吟 in BaZi and it is also known as the "Warning" Pillar. It is an indication of sad events or painful emotional situations.

An individual may encounter the Heaven and Earth Unity if it appears in their BaZi Natal Chart in either the Year, Month, or Hour, the Luck Pillars, or the Annual Pillar.

If the Heaven and Earth Unity configuration is found in the Year Pillar, the individual is likely to feel a lack of affinity with their grandparents. It may be that they struggle to relate to their grandparents and that the relationship is quite cold and distant, it is equally possible that they may never have met their grandparents.

If this configuration is visible in the Month Pillar, the individual may instead feel a lack of affinity with their parents. The relationship is likely to be rather strained and they won't be able to communicate effectively, it is possible that they may have stopped communicating altogether.

A position here could also suggest that the individual is unable to take on the family business or that they have been passed over for inheritance.

In the Hour Pillar, this configuration suggests a lack of affinity with children. It is possible that the individual may not have children or that they have been separated from their children who may be being raised in a separate household. Alternatively it may be that the individual is experiencing problems with their fertility.

If this configuration is discovered in the Luck Pillar, there are spiritual implications. This individual might spend much of their life in spiritual exploration. They may be devoutly religious or even choose to follow a religious vocation. This position may alternatively suggest that the individual will become very focused on their health, diet and physical fitness. Sadly it is also possible that they will lose a parent.

In the Year Pillar, this configuration suggests that success in work matters will be over-shadowed by sorrow or loss. The individual will progress in their careers and they will see a corresponding increase in their material wealth. They may choose to invest in property. Their achievements may however prove to be of little consolation in the face of emotionally straining events.

Metal Ox

Heaven and Earth Combine 天地相合
Xin Chou 辛丑 (Metal Ox) + Bing Zi 丙子 (Fire Rat)

This Heaven and Earth Combine Pillar is the most desirable Pillar. It is an indication that the individual will have the ability to form positive connections with all the people around them. These connections will have an impact on all the areas of their life. Individuals will this configuration in their chart, are almost certainly going to be happy and successful.

When this Pillar is found in the Chart of someone connected to the Xin Chou, it is likely that this person will be a good friend and a good influence. They may be able to offer help and support in times of need.

An individual may encounter the Heaven and Earth Combine if it appears in their BaZi Natal Chart in either the Year, Month, or Hour, the Luck Pillars, or the Annual Pillar.

If the Heaven and Earth Combine appears in the Year Pillar, the individual is likely to be close to their grandparents. They will appreciate their wisdom and will find peace in their company. It is also likely that these individuals will enjoy the support of loyal friends and that they will also have a wide social circle and a good social status.

If this configuration is found in the Month Pillar, the individual is likely to have a strong bond with their parents. They will benefit from a firm foundation and good family values. They are also likely to progress quickly in their careers as they will have the professional regard of their managers and supervisors and they will feel passionate about what they do.

In the Hour Pillar, this configuration suggests that the individual will be a good parent and that they will have a warm and understanding relationship with their children. The individual is also likely to be able to put their skills to good use as a manager and they will appreciate the support and respect of their employees.

If this configuration is visible in the Luck Pillar or the Annual Pillar, it indicates that the individual will build successful relationships in all areas of their lives. They will have a harmonious marriage and a happy home and they are also likely to achieve career success through working partnerships and joint ventures.

Rob Wealth Goat Blade 劫财羊刃
Xin Chou 辛丑 (Metal Ox) + Geng Xu 庚戌 (Metal Dog)

If you are a Xin Chou, you do not want to see a Geng Xu 庚戌 Pillar in your Chart. This will form a Rob Wealth Goat Blade 劫财羊刃 formation which is an indication of serious financial losses and emotional or relationship problems. People who have this configuration in their Chart may find that they struggle to achieve their goals. No matter how hard they work they may achieve very little and be left feeling exhausted and demoralized.

The Xin Chou individual should note that anyone connected to them with this Pillar in their Chart may be a cause of them losing money. It will not be that they will attempt to take their money and it is likely that neither party will be aware of the effect at the time. The Xin Chou may well be quite happy to see the money go. It is possible that these individuals may be the source of poor advice but it is just as likely that the Xin Chou will simply enjoy their company and be more inclined to overspend when they are together.

辛卯

Xin Mao

辛丑	辛卯	辛巳	辛未	辛酉	辛亥
Xin Chou	Xin Mao	Xin Si	Xin Wei	Xin You	Xin Hai

Getting to Know
Xin Mao 辛卯 (Metal Rabbit)

Negative Imagery

Getting to Know
辛卯 (Metal Rabbit)

General Observations:

The Xin Mao is represented by the metal of antique watches or trophies that are valuable but also fragile. Such imagery refers to individuals who have high principles in life.

The Xin Mao 辛卯 are naturally authoritative, hardworking and ambitious. They march to the beat of their own drum and are firm believers in standing up for what is right. They enjoy power and have no trouble taking the lead in situations. This works out perfectly in their favour when they are trying to achieve their goals.

Innately strong-willed and persistent, they constantly strive to make a difference in their immediate environment.

From a very early age, Xin Mao individuals understand that firmness and perseverance are the qualities that will bring lasting success into their life. They have incredible energy and stamina. All this comes from a strong mind and will power. Pursuing new, creative and innovative endeavours such as starting their own business, or pursuing a career in sports drives them to find success.

These individuals are clearly recognizable in the workplace because they are likely reaching outstanding achievements. When it comes to mapping out strategies, Xin Mao individuals are very meticulous and thorough. Through their dedicated efforts, they are the ones likely climbing the corporate ladder and progressing rapidly in their careers. They are not afraid of the pitfalls along the way. They can bounce right back up on their feet despite setbacks. They are likely to achieve outstanding success in life as a result.

They manage to take the hardships from their youth and turn it into viable wisdom for their future. For this reason, they become adept at financial planning and are able to prudently handle their personal finances.

Their proud and hardworking nature can make others feel not needed and unwanted, and this inadvertently pushes people away. In the end, they are likely to have many estranged relationships. They do not trust others easily because they find it hard to open up or to appear vulnerable to them. They need to learn that accepting help from people is not a sign of weakness and should not be overly critical about it.

Young Xin Mao individuals can often harbour insecurity. This can be self-destructive and will definitely deter them from reaching their full potential as they grow older, especially if they do not attempt to overcome this self-doubt sooner. They must learn to embrace their capabilities with confidence and have faith in themselves to move forward.

They can also come across as patronizing and insensitive due to their blunt speech and acerbic tongue. They have to remember that there is a thin line between wit and sarcasm. Failure to hold their tongue in certain situations can be costly to the Xin Mao in various areas of their life. This tactlessness can be attributed to their scepticism and doubt towards others, or they wield it as a form of self-preservation to shield them from hurt. Ultimately, they may offend and repel people, projecting a façade that others find unwelcoming when in fact, the truth is otherwise.

This distrust of others is not completely their fault. It is likely that in the past, many people around them had either betrayed or took advantage of them and their kindness. Such bad experiences had embedded into their minds, breeding insecurity overtime, which is why it takes a longer time to earn that trust in them.

Key Character Traits of the Xin Mao 辛卯: Overall

- Hardworking
- Hardworking
- Good at Strategy
- Adaptable
- Good endurance
- Impatient
- Quick Witted
- Organized

Work Life

辛卯
Xin
Mao

Professional Self

Xin Mao individuals have an ever-flowing supply of creativity and ingenuity. Couple these traits along with their independence and hard work, and you have the perfect recipe for career success.

They have strong reasoning skills, which makes them ideal in the fields of education and administration. On the other hand, their take-charge personality makes them excellent managers and supervisors. Moreover, they possess a natural executive ability and an innate understanding of the business world.

Xin Mao individuals are particularly intellectual and quick witted, which is why they require careers that offer stimulation and growth. Being involved in careers that challenge their imagination are best. They should never allow themselves to fall into repetitive and mundane routines.

As they are naturally energetic, Xin Maos are born with good endurance and stamina - qualities that are sought after in sports. This makes them likely to excel in their chosen athletic field, as they are driven to push themselves physically and mentally to the next level. With such determination, they can become highly paid athletes.

Congenial working atmospheres are necessary in order for the Xin Mao to feel happy and content. Stress and strife does not work well for them. If they have trouble getting along with co-workers or supervisors, they are likely to look for a career elsewhere.

Career Options

Metal Rabbit

Individuals born under this Pillar are highly astute and detailed. Their investigative and analytical tendencies would make them excellent detectives, and private investigators. These same qualities would also serve them well as lawyers or magistrates.

Pursuing a career in creative writing would also be ideal because they could use their active imagination to create compelling and entertaining stories. They could also use their creative abilities in the career realms of art or design.

Due to their independent thinking and love for knowledge, they would also make excellent educators. Furthermore, they have a love for helping and motivating others, which is why careers that include teaching, coaching, training and healing are also ideal.

Metal Rabbit

Key Character Traits of the Xin Mao 辛卯: Work life

Positive

- Good Planner
- Individual Thinker
- Considerate
- Agreeable
- Tactful
- Thoughtful

Negative

- Moody
- Lack of Confidence
- Selfish
- Suspicious
- Detached
- Stubborn

Love and Relationships

Xin Mao

Love

Individuals born under this Pillar are attracted to powerful, successful and influential people. Being in the company of an interesting or unusual partner is important for keeping the Xin Mao's interest.

When it comes to love, relationships and commitment, the Xin Mao can be extremely indecisive. Long term commitments do not appeal to the Xin Mao because they have a need for change and variety in their lives.

They will want to travel and meet people beyond their own social group. For this reason, it is a struggle for them to settle down with one person and may spend many years in and out of relationships.

When they do find that special one, they are generous and willing to make sacrifices for their partner.

Acquaintances

Being around a wide variety of positive people is important for the Xin Mao. They require stimulating company and enjoy socializing with those who are also ambitious and aspiring. As natural entertainers, they are witty, hilarious and rarely feel out of place. It is important for them to be around others who will appreciate their vibrant personalities.

Others are quick to admit how loyal and caring the Xin Mao are. They are excellent friends and trustworthy confidants who are willing to help anyone in need.

Family

For the most part, they are committed to their families and are able to lead them in a positive direction. Best described as a voice of reason, they are always working for peace and harmony in their relationships.

Because of their loyalty, they will sometimes allow themselves to be the martyr. They must be careful of this as they may allow themselves to be taken advantage of.

Although they are devoted to their family, they do have an urge to venture out and explore. If they do not get this fulfilment, they will feel stifled. This in turn will clash with their family life.

Metal Rabbit

Key Character Traits of the Xin Mao 辛卯: Love & Relationships

- Relationships in many different social groups
- Desire for Peace and Harmony
- Potential for martyrdom
- Attracted to Power and Creativity
- Need Intimacy
- Potential Sexual Issues

Famous Personalities

Michael Jordan - Former American professional basketball player, and is acclaimed as one of the greatest basketball player of all time. He is an entrepreneur and majority owner and chairman of the Charlotte Bobcats.

Albert Finney - English actor. He has appeared in numerous plays and films to-date, and has been active in the industry since 1958.

Source: Wikipedia (June 2013)

Technical Analysis

Xin Mao

BaZi Day Pillar Analytics 日柱分析

時 Hour	日 Day	月 Month	年 Year	
	辛 Xin **Yin Metal** (DM)			Heavenly Stems 天干
	卯 Mao **Rabbit** Yin Wood (Extinction 絕)			Earthly Branches 地支
	乙 Yi - Wood 才 IW			Hidden Stems 藏干

辛卯 Metal Rabbit

Description

This Xin 辛 Metal sits on the Indirect Wealth Star 偏財星, which is also a Peach Blossom Star 桃花星. This setup indicates an individual who is beautiful and charming with a romantic nature, but may struggle with long term commitments in relationships.

The Xin Mao individual often presents quite a serious demeanour. They are rather reserved and, although they are fond of people and socialising, they are often quite detached and introspective.

With an interest in facts and figures, the Xin Mao individual likes to take their time to really examine an issue before reaching a conclusion. Shrewd and analytical and also very practical and adaptable, they are able to apply their skills to a variety of tasks and endeavours.

Metal Rabbit

Though they are very reserved, the Xin Mao, nevertheless, has very good people skills. Thanks to the *hidden-pull* of the Xu 戌 (Dog) Branch which contains the Friend Star 比肩星, they are often able to move easily through different social groups, making connections with individuals from all walks of life. Intuitive, sensitive and understanding, they are also very diplomatic. This is because the Xu 戌 (Dog) also contains a Direct Resource Star 正印星. They like to feel that they are part of a group and they enjoy, and often benefit from, group activities where they are able to interact, leverage off and learn from others.

Although they may be very gifted with the written word, the Xin Mao may sometimes struggle to express themselves verbally. Through developing their communication skills, they may be able to cultivate a deeper sense of independence and establish self-confidence. This is because of the clash between Metal and Wood of this Pillar. Very easily hurt by criticism, they are often very doubtful of their abilities and they can be indecisive and inclined to over-thinking before making their choice. They can also be very dependent on their loved ones for emotional support and validation. If they learn to trust their instincts and have more faith in themselves, they will be able to become more assertive.

Technical Observations

Metal Rabbit

As the Pillar is seated on the Wealth 財星 Star, Xin Mao individuals are often stylish and elegant. The Clash between the Metal-Wood of this Pillar indicates that they are sensitive and quite emotionally vulnerable. Though they may have the ability to develop friendships and move comfortably in social situations, they are often quite fragile and lonely deep inside. It is favourable for this Pillar if it is assisted and supported by the positive presence of Wu Zi 戊子, Wu Xu 戊戌 or Bing Xu 丙戌 at the Stem and Branches. This combination helps give them more confidence, and is often an indication that they will marry into money or that they will enjoy wealth and fame though their hard work and perseverance.

It is inauspicious if this Pillar is only supported by Stems, Bing 丙 and Ding 丁 in their BaZi Chart. It is often also best for them to avoid excessive Water 水 or Fire 火 elements, especially with the presence of additional Hai 亥 (Pig) and Mao 卯 (Rabbit), as these can distort the individual's capabilities.

If the individual was born during the day time (5AM - 5PM), they are likely to have a happy marriage without too much friction. Those born during the night time (5PM - 5AM) may, however, find it hard to maintain a long term relationship. Those individuals born during the Chou 丑 (Ox) month may not have the best of luck in life, they may find that their investments fail to be fruitful and that they face many challenges on their career paths.

Unique 60 Pillar Combinations

This section covers the relationships between the individual pillar under this elemental polarity and several other pillars found in the 60 Jia Zi cycle.

Xin
Mao

Na Yin Death and Extinct 納音死絕
Xin Mao 辛卯 (Metal Rabbit) + Bing Shen 丙申 (Fire Monkey)

The Na Yin 納音 is known as the Melodic Element of a Pillar. The Na Yin influences the subconscious mind of an individual. This can affect how a person feels, perceives or even remembers information and past experiences.

If the Na Yin Death and Extinct Pillar is formed when the Xin Mao meets with the Bing Shen, it may be found at either the Year, Month, or Hour Pillars, as well as, the Luck Pillar and Annual Pillar.

If this configuration is found in the Year Pillar of the individual's Natal Chart, it indicates that they will feel a lack of affinity with their grandparents. They are likely to have quite a distant relationship, they will not be emotionally close and the relationship may even be completely severed. This is possible even if they live in close proximity.

If this configuration is visible in the Month Pillar, the individual will, instead, feel a lack of affinity with their parents. The individual is likely to struggle to be able to connect with their parents intellectually or emotionally. It is possible that they may not be on speaking terms. The Month Pillar also represents career and placement here suggests that the individual has been unable to find career that inspires them and they are not engaged with their career path. Equally it could be that they are unhappy at work and that they do not feel they are achieving.

In the Hour Pillar, this configuration suggests a lack of affinity with children. This could be an indication that the individual's children are being brought up by a previous partner. Alternatively the individual may be bringing up children who are not biologically their own due to marriage or adoption. The Hour Pillar is also connected to ideas and contributions. In this position the individual may feel quite philosophically lost and they will be uncertain of their purpose and how they can go about giving something back to society.

Metal Rabbit

When this configuration is present in the Luck Pillar, the individual is likely to live through a decade in which they are unable to access their intuition. They are likely to be quite indecisive and uncertain; they may feel that they are always making the wrong choices and misinterpreting events and situations. This could understandably result in some anxiety and upset, these individuals would be wise to turn to trusted friends and family for help.

If this configuration is found in the Annual Pillar, the individual is likely to feel uncertain and anxious, they will worry a great deal but they will not be able to locate the source of their feelings. They would again be wise to seek support from their loved ones.

Heaven Combine Earth Punish 天合地刑
Xin Mao 辛卯 (Metal Rabbit) + Bing Zi 丙子 (Fire Rat)

In this configuration, the Day Pillar and Bing Zi 丙子 Combine with the Heavenly Stem but form a Punishment 刑 with the Earthly Branch in the Chart. With this configuration, the appearance of the Heavenly Stem would appear to indicate a positive outlook, but as the Earthly Branch forms a Punishment, the indications are that the individual will be plagued with feelings of tension, emotional pain, and stress. In this situation it is likely that the individual will gloss over their negative emotions and put on a show of happiness.

An individual may encounter the Heaven Combine Earth Punish Pillar if it appears in their BaZi Natal Chart at either the Year, Month, or Hour Pillars, as well as, the Luck Pillar and Annual Pillar.

If this configuration is found in the Year Pillar, the indications are that an outwardly favourable relationship with the individual's grandparents is nothing more than a disguise. Under the surface there will be a great deal of tension and unhappiness.

If this configuration is visible in the Month Pillar, the individual may appear to enjoy a warm and pleasant relationship with their parents, but though they may play their part well, their true feelings will be far more complicated and the relationship will be far less happy than it seems. A position here can also suggest problems with office politics. The individual will smile and be pleasant in the workplace but they will be consumed by fears over the conversations that may be being had behind closed doors and they will worry about their position within the team. On this occasion the individual needs to think through the reasons behind their reactions and emotions. It is very likely that they are the source of their own distress and that they need to learn to relax and have faith in their colleagues.

Metal Rabbit

In the Hour Pillar, this configuration suggests that the individual may have a tendency to make empty promises. They will over commit without following through and leave their friends and colleagues disappointed leading ultimately to issues of trust. It will be important for these people to learn to be more assertive and only take on the tasks they know they can complete.

When this configuration is found in the Luck Pillar, it is suggests a situation in which all may appear to working in the individual's favour. They will be very successful and they will have earned the respect and the admiration of their friends and colleagues. Despite all this they will lack faith in themselves, they will not believe that they deserve their good fortune and they may begin to sabotage their own progress. They need to work on their self-confidence.

If this configuration occurs in the Annual Pillar it is possible that promising deals worked on throughout the year will fall apart at the last minute. The year may appear to be tortured by tension and mistrust and the individual is likely to lose confidence. They are advised to remain calm and not to allow their fears to get the better of them. It is likely that it will be their own anxiety and last minute meddling that will cause their plans to go off track.

Heaven Combine Earth Harm 天合地害
Xin Mao 辛卯 (Metal Rabbit) + Bing Chen 丙辰 (Fire Dragon)

In this configuration, the Bing Chen 丙辰 and the Day Pillar combine with the Heavenly Stem, but form a Harm 害 with the Earthly Branch. Again, the outlook for the individual would seem to be very positive on the surface, but they will be hiding their uncertainty about their relationships and they may, at times, fear betrayal.

An individual may encounter Heaven Combine Earth Harm Pillar if it appears in their BaZi Natal Chart at either the Year, Month, or Hour Pillars, as well as, the Luck Pillar and Annual Pillar.

If this configuration is found in the Year Pillar, the individual is likely to appear to have a perfectly pleasant relationship with their grandparents but they will nevertheless be insecure about the connection and they may not be sure that they can trust their grandparents. Alternatively it may be their friends that are not be trustworthy and the individual may fear that they are being talked about behind their backs.

In the Month Pillar, this configuration suggests problems in the individual's relationship with their parents. They may appear to have a good relationship with their parents but in reality they will be quite unsure about whether their parents would stand by them in a crisis. Alternatively it may be the individual's relationship with their supervisors and managers at work that is uncertain, they may feel unsupported by their managers and their colleagues may leave them to carry an unfair work load.

If this configuration is found in the Hour Pillars, the individual may fear that their children are not being completely honest with them. Alternatively they may not have the loyalty of their staff and may find it hard to develop a stable team.

In the Luck Pillars, this configuration indicates that the individual may appear to achieve a great deal but they will be left with a bad taste in their mouth. They are likely to feel that their success has come at a cost to them and they have been abused or victimised in some way. No amount of financial reward will change their feelings.

If this configuration is found in the Annual Pillar, it suggests that a promising a year will end in disappointment. It is likely that the individual will allow their judgement to be distorted by jealousy and that this will change their perception of their accomplishments. It will be important for them to remember that the grass isn't always greener and they need to stop comparing their accomplishments with others.

Heaven Friend Earth Clash 天比地冲
Xin Mao 辛卯 (Metal Rabbit) + Xin You 辛酉 (Metal Rooster)

When the Xin You 辛酉 and the Day Pillar form the Heaven Friend Earth Clash, it indicates that an early agreement will fall part and escalate into arguments and discord due to a change in plans or circumstances. It is also likely that individuals with this Pillar in their Chart will be frequently very active with very busy schedules but they will achieve very little with all their efforts. Situations that seemed promising in the beginning are likely to end with displeasure and dissatisfaction.

That is not to say that the implications of this configuration are always bad. The ultimate outcome will be depend on whether the Heavenly Stem is favourable, if this is the case then even an apparently negative turn of events may yet prove to have a beneficial effect in the long term.

An individual may encounter Heaven Friend Earth Clash Pillar if it appears in their BaZi Natal Chart at either the Year, Month, or Hour Pillars, as well as, the Luck Pillar and Annual Pillar.

If this configuration is found in any of the Year, Month, or Hour Pillars, it suggests that these events and emotions will play out in connection to the individuals various relationships. Found in the Year Pillar, it will be the individual's relationships with their grandparents that is affected, either due to friction or that they may have never met. As the Year Pillar also represents one's social circle, it is likely that this individual has a more detached relationship with his/her friends and may suffer from the lack of support.

The Month Pillar represents a person's work and career aspects in life. If this configuration appears here, it will affect the individual's relationship with their employers, which could impede his/her career prospects in the long run. It will also influence the individual's affinity to his/her parents as a misunderstanding could be the root to their estranged connection.

Metal Rabbit

In the Hour Pillar, this configuration will affect their relationship with their children, employees and clients. In each case some unexpected news or a change in plans or circumstances will have the effect of destabilising the relationship and causing conflict. It could be that the individual is made redundant, or that they have to travel for work. They may separate from their partner or begin a new relationship. It has to be noted that although the relationships may appear to be negatively impacted at first, if the Heavenly Stem is positive, the individual may ultimately find that the relationships are enhanced and improved by the change in circumstances.

If this configuration is seen in the Luck Pillars, the individual is likely to experience a period of steady change in their lives and perspectives. The individual may live through some difficult times. There is an indication that process may even be a painful one. Ultimately, the progress and growth that come about will be a positive.

If this configuration is found in the Annual Pillar, it suggests a year of surprises. This may not be an easy year; it is likely to be confusing and unsettling. There will be a great deal of unexpected events which will change the individual's life and also their inner landscape. They will have to face some private struggles as they attempt to reconcile the emotions that surface in response to each new situation but it will all prove to be a valuable learning experience and the individual will emerge enriched by self-discovery.

Heaven and Earth Clash 天冲地冲
Xin Mao 辛卯 (Metal Rabbit) + Ding You 丁酉 (Fire Rooster)

 +

This Heaven and Earth Clash Pillar is a configuration in which the Day Pillar is clashed by the Ding You 丁酉 Pillar. This is known as the Fan Yin 反吟 formation and it is an unlucky formation as it will act to diminish any of the good qualities of an individual's Day Pillar. In addition to impairing the individual's chances of success by impacting upon their abilities, this Pillar may also place more obstacles in their path.

As with the Rob Wealth Goat Blade, this configuration may have an impact on the Xin Mao even if it appears in someone else's Chart. On this occasion these individuals are likely to be a bad influence on the Xin Mao's career. Again they are unlikely to be setting out to hold the Xin Mao back but they might be the source of poor advice or simply a distraction.

Seen in the Natal Chart, this configuration indicates a lack of affinity with the individual or concept represented by the specific Pillar in which it appears.

If this configuration is seen in the Year Pillar, the individual is likely to experience a lack of affinity with their grandparents. It is possible that they may feel that the gap between the generations is too wide to cross and they may be unable to see eye to eye. It may also be that these individuals may struggle to make friends. They may be quite shy and insecure.

When this configuration is found in the Month Pillar, the individual is likely to feel a lack of affinity with their parents. It may be that they disagree on major issues or that their goals and perspectives in life are widely disparate. As hard as they try they are unable to form a profound connection. Alternatively the individual may not be able to build a positive working relationship with their managers and colleagues at work.

In the Hour Pillar, the individual is likely to feel a lack of affinity with their children, it could be that they struggle to understand their children, or that they are unable to spend enough time with them to really get to know them. Alternatively they may not be able to relate to their staff and employees. A position in the Hour Pillar could also be an indication that the individual feels a little lost, they may not know their true place in the world and they may lack for a feeling of purpose.

Where this configuration is present in the Luck Pillar, the individual is likely to face a period of time in which they have many challenges to face and obstacles to overcome. They may feel that no matter where they turn, there is another barrier in their way, and that nothing is turning out as they planned. They are advised to fall back on the love and support of their friends and families.

In the Annual Pillar, this configuration is an indication that the individual may not enjoy the very best of luck for the year. They are recommended to avoid making any serious decisions or significant changes where possible. They should also refrain from becoming involved in any major financial investments.

Heaven Counter Earth Clash 天剋地沖
Xin Mao 辛卯 (Metal Rabbit) + Yi You 乙酉 (Wood Rooster)

This Heaven Counter Earth Clash Pillar is a configuration in which the Day Pillar is going against the Yi You 乙酉. It is important to note that this configuration and the Heaven and Earth Clash formation are different. In this situation the individual of this Pillar is in control and far from being diminished, they are empowered. They will have passion and a strong desire to win. They are likely to be dominant characters with an entrepreneurial spirit who have a great deal of potential to achieve significant success but they must be careful not to be impatient or over hasty in their decision making.

An individual may encounter this Heaven Counter Earth Clash Pillar if it appears in their Natal Chart in either the Year, Month, or Hour Pillar, as well as the Luck Pillars, or the Annual Pillar.

When this configuration is seen in the Year Pillar, it suggests that the individual will benefit from the assistance of friends in high places. These people may be able to offer the Xin Mao useful advice and good guidance but it will not be a substitute for hard work.

It this configuration is found in the Month Pillar, the individual is likely to have a flair for business and they will be very money minded. They may need to guard against their love of turning a profit becoming an obsession and their motives being driven by greed.

When found in the Hour Pillar, this configuration suggests that the individual will be married to their work. They will work all the hours they have available to them and they are unlikely to spare much time for their friends and family. These individuals may need to be reminded that they have a responsibility to their loved ones as much as to their career path.

In the Luck Pillar, this configuration suggests that the individual will have the drive and the ability to pursue career development and material wealth. They are likely to have a great skill for business and an eye for an investment. They are advised to make the most of the chances they get to pursue their goals but they should not be impatient and they should think clearly before making a decision.

When this configuration occurs in the Annual Pillar, the individual will have a very positive year in terms of career progression and investment. They may become involved in new business ventures and they are very likely to see an improvement in their financial situation. Though they are advised to make the most of every opportunity that comes their way, they are also reminded to look to their health and their family's wellbeing. Though the year will be fruitful, it will also be stressful and the individual's personal relationships may come under strain.

Heaven and Earth Unity 天同地比
Xin Mao 辛卯 (Metal Rabbit) + Xin Mao 辛卯 (Metal Rabbit)

The Heaven and Earth Unity Pillar is traditionally known as the Fu Yin 伏吟 formation in BaZi. It is considered the hidden warning Pillar and it is, sadly, an indication of sorrow and distressing events.

An individual may encounter Heaven and Earth Unity Pillar if it appears in their BaZi Natal Chart at either the Year, Month, or Hour Pillars, as well as, the Luck Pillar and Annual Pillar.

If this configuration is found in the Year Pillar, there are poor indications for the individual's connection with their grandparents. The relationship may be under some considerable emotional strain, it is equally possible however that the individual may never have met their grandparents.

In the Month Pillar, this configuration carries implications for the individual's relationship with their parents. They may struggle to be able to relate to their parents at all and they will not be able to communicate effectively. There are also indications of potential troubles with inheritance. It could be that their parents are unable or unwilling to pass on a family business or some property.

Metal Rabbit

If this configuration appears in the Hour Pillar, the individual is likely to have a weak affinity with children. It may be that they do not have children, either by choice or it may be that they are experiencing problems with their fertility. Alternatively their children could have been separated from them.

In the Luck Pillar, this configuration indicates a spiritual path. This individual may dedicate their life to religion. Alternatively they may become very focused on their health, and will devote a significant amount of time to their diet, exercise and physical well-being. Sadly there is also a possibility that they may lose, or have lost, a parent.

When this configuration is found in the Annual Pillar, the individual is likely to experience a very positive year in terms of career, achievement and financial wealth. They may be promoted or invest in property. They may become involved in a new working partnership or a successful new venture. They will also have to face with at least one emotionally challenging event.

Heaven and Earth Combine 天地相合
Xin Mao 辛卯 (Metal Rabbit) + Bing Xu 丙戌 (Fire Dog)

The Heaven and Earth Combine Pillar is the most desirable Pillar. This Pillar is an indication of great connectivity and affinity. The individual will enjoy positive relationships in all areas of their life and they are likely to be very successful and very happy as a result.

Even when found in another individual's Chart the Xin Mao will still feel the effects. Anyone with this Pillar in their Chart is likely to prove to have a positive impact on the Xin Mao's life.

A person may encounter Heaven and Earth Combine Pillar if it appears in their BaZi Natal Chart at either the Year, Month, or Hour Pillars, as well as, the Luck Pillar and Annual Pillar.

If this configuration is found in the Year Pillar, the individual will appreciate the comfort and wisdom offered by their grandparents. They are also likely to have a high social status and benefit from a variety of connections and an interesting and active social life.

If you find this configuration in the Month Pillar, the individual is likely to have an excellent relationship with their parents. The will have the confidence that comes from a secure foundation and the assurance of support and guidance when they need it. They are also likely to have a positive working relationship with their managers and supervisor that will help them to progress quickly in their careers.

In the Hour Pillar, this configuration is an indication that the individual will be able to bring up their children in a secure and happy home. They will have an open and loving relationship. Equally they are likely to benefit from the loyalty of a steadfast team of employees who will always work to the best of their abilities.

If this configuration is found in either the Luck Pillar or the Annual Pillar, it denotes successful relationships that create positivity in all areas of the individual's life. They will become wealthy through joint ventures and cooperative endeavours. They will be lucky in love and happy in marriage.

Mutual Exchange Goat Blade 互換羊刃
Xin Mao 辛卯 (Metal Rabbit) + Jia Xu 甲戌 (Wood Dog)

The Xin Mao meets with a Jia Xu 甲戌 Pillar is called the Mutual Exchange Goat Blade 互換羊刃 Pillar. This has a similar effect to meeting with a Rob Wealth Goat Blade 劫財羊刃. However in this situation the impact is felt upon the individual's health. They might face circumstances that cause their health to deteriorate or they may be involved in accidents. Their chances of being involved in an accident may be increased if they are in the company of another individual with this formation in their Chart.

Rob Wealth Goat Blade 劫財羊刃
Xin Mao 辛卯 (Metal Rabbit) + Geng Xu 庚戌 (Metal Dog)

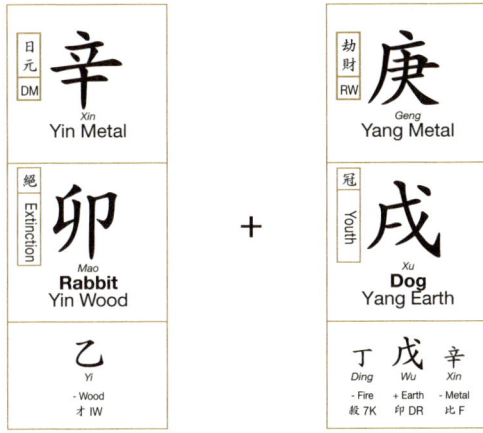

If you are a Xin Mao, you do not want to see a Geng Xu 庚戌 Pillar in your Chart. This will form a Rob Wealth Goat Blade 劫財羊刃 formation, which is an indication of serious financial losses and emotional or relationship problems. People who have this configuration in their Chart may find life tough. They may be left feeling exhausted as goals appear ever elusive.

Anyone connected to the Xin Mao with this Pillar in their Chart may be the cause of them losing money. It should not be assumed that this is intentional on their part. That is likely to be far from being the case and is it, in fact, possible that neither party will be aware of the effect at the time. It may be that the Xin Mao is simply very fond of this person and that they are inclined to spend money on them or on trying to impress them. They may be quite happy to spend the money at the time.

己巳	己未	己酉	己亥	己丑	己卯	己巳	己未	己酉	己亥	己丑	己卯	己巳
己未	己酉	己亥	己丑	己卯	己巳	己未	己酉	己亥	己丑	己卯	己巳	己未
己酉	己亥	己丑	己卯	己巳	己未	己酉	己亥	己丑	己卯	己巳	己未	己酉
己亥	己丑	己卯	己巳	己未	己酉	己亥	己丑	己卯	己巳	己未	己酉	己亥
己丑	己卯	己巳	己未	己酉	己亥	己丑	己卯	己巳	己未	己酉	己亥	己丑
己卯	己巳	己未	己酉	己亥	己丑	己卯	己巳	己未	己酉	己亥	己丑	己卯
己巳	己未	己酉	己亥	己丑	己卯	己巳	己未	己酉	己亥	己丑	己卯	己巳
己未	己酉	己亥	己丑	己卯	己巳	己未	己酉	己亥	己丑	己卯	己巳	己未
己酉	己亥	己丑	己卯	己巳	己未	己酉	己亥	己丑	己卯	己巳	己未	己酉
己亥	己丑	己卯	己巳	己未	己酉	己亥	己丑	己卯	己巳	己未	己酉	己亥
己丑	己卯	己巳	己未	己酉	己亥	己丑	己卯	己巳	己未	己酉	己亥	己丑
己卯	己巳	己未	己酉	己亥	己丑	己卯	己巳	己未	己酉	己亥	己丑	己卯

辛巳
Xin Si

辛丑 辛卯 辛巳 辛未 辛酉 辛亥
Xin Chou | Xin Mao | Xin Si | Xin Wei | Xin You | Xin Hai

Getting to Know
Xin Si 辛巳 (Metal Snake)

Metal
Snake

Positive Imagery

Negative Imagery

辛巳 Metal Snake

Getting to Know
Xin Si 辛巳 (Metal Snake)

General Observations:

The image of raw jade visually represents the Xin Si Pillar, which reflects exquisiteness and sophistication. Xin Si 辛巳 individuals are born with beauty and grace. Others immediately recognize them, which is why they are often able to rely on their good looks in order to get ahead in life. They carry themselves in a classy way and exude charisma, elegance and sophistication.

Xin Si individuals are very conscious of the way they look and take time to create a favourable image. In the long run, they desire to seize the approval of others. This vying for approval turns out great because Xin Si individuals are typically popular and well-received.

Don't be mistaken; Xin Si individuals are more than just a pretty face. They are actually witty, intelligent and perseverant. They are quick-thinking and are usually able to act swiftly when the occasion arises. In addition to being witty, they are also creative. There is a strong desire within the Xin Si to do something original and outside of the box. In order to find success, they channel their good traits to focus on whatever matter is at hand.

Life is good to them in many areas. Not only are they good looking, they also enjoy a good life full of bountiful blessings and resources. They are extremely successful at accumulating money and assets. Once they learn not to take their luck for granted, they can easily reach their full potential in life.

They never have to look far for help in life. Whenever they are faced with an obstacle, help is always close. People will always be nearby willing to provide guidance and assistance for them. Others are so willing to help them because of their warm and friendly demeanour. They communicate well with others and are always viewed as relatable.

Sometimes they are known to be tense and nervous, especially after they may have taken on too much. They are also highly impatient, and will often focus their energy on the larger picture, instead of the details. By not paying attention to the details, they can lower their chances for success.

Metal Snake

Many of these issues are indications that they need to balance. Balancing will cause them to avoid many obstacles and pitfalls in in life. Because they are interested in so many different areas, they may spread themselves too thin. Spreading themselves too thin will keep them imbalanced and increase their stress levels.

As they may appear to be rather scatter-brained - probably because they want to do everything all at once - they tend to have a hard time making any decisions or setting priorities on what needs to be done. If they do not learn to commit to a decision, they risk zapping out their energy and in the end, things would be left unfinished or that they are unable to deliver what they promised on time. This will ultimately make them seem unreliable to others. It is advised that they find ways to calm their minds so that they can reflect and make better decisions.

Metal Snake

The Xin Si must also maintain a watchful eye on their finances. Their love for the good things in life may lead to over-indulgence if they are not in control of their expenses. They need to avoid frivolous spending and be more calculative when it comes to investments.

Key Character Traits of the Xin Si 辛巳: Overall

- Attractive
- Compassionate
- Talented
- Self-Doubting
- Lucky
- In Need of Others' Approval
- Charming

Work Life

辛巳

Xin Si

Professional Self

Xin Si individuals are intellectually insightful, which enables them to be successful in any career they choose. However, they are happiest when they hold positions where they are able to work on their own terms such as being self-employed or as a freelancer.

They have impeccable skills when it comes to dealing with other people. This can lead them into career fields involving healing, or alternative health. This same desire to help others may also lead them into non-profit and charitable organizations.

Although they desire leadership roles, they may lack the self-confidence to make this happen. Doubt and indecision can hinder them from achieving their careers goals.

Career Options

The Xin Si will find most careers fulfilling and satisfying. There are several options available for them. All they have to do is make up their minds to pursue it.

They do not like to take orders from others and should avoid careers where they are unable to be their own boss. Because of this, self-employment, entrepreneurship, and management are ideal.

Careers where the Xin Si can help other people will bring them the most satisfaction in life. This innate desire to help others would make them suitable for vocations in psychology or counselling. Some may desire to heal others. In these cases, they would do well in the medical field.

Xin Si individuals are also great evaluators, which would cause them to excel in business, commerce, or real estate.

Known for their graceful physical movements and nimble body, they are likely to perform well in physical art or sports like gymnastics, dance, martial arts, yoga and even modelling. They may even find fame in such fields.

Some Xin Si's have a burning desire to explore and travel. These individuals would do well working abroad.

Metal Snake

Key Character Traits of the Xin Si 辛巳: Work life

Positive

- Creative
- Strong Convictions
- Humanitarian
- Dependable
- Hardworking
- Competitive
- Independent
- Optimistic

Negative

- Jealous
- Egotistical
- Selfish
- Unstable
- Discontented
- Impatient
- Resentful

Love and Relationships

Xin
Si

Love

Xin Si individuals have an interest in self-improvement and are attracted to people who have a desire to better themselves as well. They also look for partners who are ambitious and mentally stimulating. Overall, they have high expectations for their relationships.

Because they are charming and good looking, they are often sought after by the opposite sex. Even though several suitors are always trying to win the Xin Si's attention, they still have a difficult time selecting a partner.

The Xin Si is an excellent communicator and can often smooth over any issues in their relationships. The only time they have major difficulties in their love life is when they allow their insecurities to surface. This will lead to arguments, strife and disagreements in the relationship.

When in relationships, they have a tendency to be critical or bossy towards their spouse. They need to be careful not to become overly jealous, possessive or suspicious.

Acquaintances

Xin Si individuals are witty and humorous. They are natural entertainers and are very enjoyable to be around. Because of this, they tend to have wide social circles with people from various walks of life. Their magnetism and charisma make them one of the more popular people in their social groups.

They also enjoy learning and sharing knowledge, and prefer to be around people who are interesting and can provide them with mental stimulation.

In every relationship, Xin Si individuals prefer to be direct and diplomatic.

Metal Snake

Family

They are devoted to their family life and make excellent spouses and parents. They will more than likely produce intelligent and well-mannered children. Additionally, their offspring tend to experience great success in their lives.

Marriage for them will bring an average amount of happiness. Most often, their love life will be a mixture of highs and lows, happiness and sorrow.

Although dedicated to their family, life can become problematic if the marriage is not harmonious.
If there is no harmony in their union, it will cause a downward spiral that is difficult to reverse.

Key Character Traits of the Xin Si 辛巳: Love & Relationships

- Sensitive and Caring
- Enjoy Stimulating Relationships
- Loves to be flattered
- Tendency Towards Jealousy
- Large Social Circles

Famous Personalities

George W. Bush - The 43rd President of United States, and the eldest son of George H. W. Bush, the 41st President of United States. He is also a businessman.

Angelina Jolie - American actress, film director and humanitarian. She is a Special Envoy for the United Nations High Commissioner for Refugees (UNHCR). She is also a mother of six children, where three were adopted from third world countries.

Charles G. Koch - American businessman and philanthropist. He is the co-owner and CEO of Koch Industries, a company he and his brother, David H. Koch, inherited from their father.

Source: Wikipedia (June 2013)

Technical Analysis

Xin
Si

BaZi Day Pillar Analytics 日柱分析

辛巳
Metal Snake

時 Hour	日 Day	月 Month	年 Year	
	辛 Xin Yin Metal (DM 日元)			天干 Heavenly Stems
	巳 Si Snake Yin Fire (Death 死)			地支 Earthly Branches
	庚 Geng +Metal RW 劫 / 丙 Bing +Fire DO 官 / 戊 Wu +Earth DR 印			藏干 Hidden Stems

Description

The Xin Si 辛巳 sits on the Direct Resource 正印星, Direct Officer 正官星, and Rob Wealth 劫財星 Stars. This Xin 辛 Metal is very auspicious. Though these individuals are often characterised as being soft and gentle, the support that they have from the Direct Resource and Rob Wealth Stars will turn any negatives into positives, particular with reference to material success. It would be an even better structure if this Day Pillar were to see the Bing 丙 Fire and the Direct Officer Star 正官星 on the Stem, as this would provide balance and stability to the Pillar. This formation indicates that the individual will be very wealthy and they will achieve a great deal in their chosen field.

The Xin Si individual is a visionary. Their minds are full of unique and original ideas and they are incredibly

Metal Snake

creative and energetic. All this thanks to the hidden Rob Wealth Star 劫財星. Often drawn to the arts and performance the Xin Si individual will use their artistic nature as means to express their deep emotions. It will be important for them to be able to develop their own ideas if they are to find happiness and fulfilment. They may also need to learn how to focus their tremendous energy if they are to be able to reach their full potential.

In balance to their creativity, the Xin Si individual also has a good business sense. They value structure and order and they will prefer to be in a position of authority in which they can be given free rein to make their own decisions. They tend to be perfectionists with a critical eye and strong opinions. They may need to work to be more persuasive than bossy if they are to get the best out of people and achieve the maximum.

Though the Xin Si person may, at times, appear to be overly opinionated and self-centred, they are also very honest and fair in their dealings. They are deeply humanitarian, very caring people, who are deeply protective of their loved ones. This is the effect of the hidden Direct Officer Star 正官星. They will be willing and able to use their innovative thinking to help others find solutions for their problems. They are quite likely, nevertheless, to frequently feel misunderstood and their sensitivity will make them very vulnerable to criticism.

The Xin Si individual values emotional security and they will have a true desire to settle down and start a family. Though they wish profoundly to make a home and be a parent they may find that they struggle to build the foundation of a happy marriage.

Technical Observations

The Xin Si will only shine when it meets with the positive presence of the Water 水 element. The best combination for them is one in which there is a favourable Water element in the Chart. It is also positive for them to meet with additional Metal 金 element. However, they need to avoid meeting with excessive Wood 木, Fire 火 and Earth 土 elements as this will dampen the quality of the Xin Si Pillar.

If the Xin Si individual was born during the night hours between 5PM and 5AM, they will tend to be very attractive in appearance. Those born in the Spring and Summer seasons are likely to have difficult childhoods, and they may come to feel that they were neglected by their parents. Due to a lack of Noble help, individuals of this Pillar will have to find success based on their own efforts and intelligence if they were born in the Autumn and Winter seasons.

Those born during the Wu 午 (Horse) month will face an uphill battle to succeed in their endeavours. They must also be watchful of their health as they are more prone to illnesses. The Xin Si born during the Chou 丑 (Ox) month, where this will form the *Half Grave-combo* 墓地半合 in the Chart, will have a lack of conviction in life and that their luck in wealth and marriage is poor. A Punishment will be formed if the Xin Si is born during the Yin 寅 (Tiger) month. This Punishment happens because the Yin 寅 (Tiger) contains the Wealth Star, which indicates poor financial luck. Those born during the months of Shen 申 (Monkey) or You 酉 (Rooster) tend to be wealthy and prosperous in life. However, they

still need to be cautious with their finances and assets as they are likely to meet with a loss of wealth at some point in their lifetime.

There will be fame and good reputation for those Xin Si born during the Zi 子 (Rat) month, as its Eating God Star 食神星 in the Chart is in a prosperous position. Similar outlook is possible for those born during the Si 巳 (Snake) month, as its Geng Metal is the Growth 長生 position for Si. However, for this outcome to happen, this Chart also needs to be able to transform the Water element effectively. The Xin Si born during the Hai 亥 (Pig) month will have a life blessed with good fortune because the Hai Clashes with the Si in the Day Branch. Those born during the Mao 卯 (Rabbit) month can expect to enjoy favourable indirect wealth luck from rewards and inheritance in their lifetime.

Unique 60 Pillar Combinations

This section covers the relationships between the individual pillar under this elemental polarity and several other pillars found in the 60 Jia Zi cycle.

Xin
Si

Heaven Combine Earth Punish 天合地刑
Xin Si 辛巳 (Metal Snake) + Bing Shen 丙申 (Fire Monkey)

The Xin Si and Bing Shen 丙申 Pillars will become a Heaven Combine Earth Punish configuration with the Earthly Branch. This configuration suggests an external appearance of happiness due to the presence of the Heavenly Stem, but the Punishment indicates that the individual's true emotions will be rather more unsettled.

An individual may encounter this Heaven Combine Earth Punish Pillar if it appears in their Natal BaZi Chart in either the Year, Month, or Hour Pillars, as well as the Luck Pillars, and the Annual Pillar.

If this configuration is found in the Year Pillar, it indicates that a tense and unhappy relationship with the individual's grandparents will be the reality behind the façade of a warm and successful connection. As the Year Pillar also governs one's social circle, this configuration here would mean that there is a sense of detachment in the relationship between this individual and his/her friends. There is also a lack of support coming from his/her friends as this individual does not have a close bond with them.

When found in the Month Pillar, this configuration suggests that the outward appearance of a positive relationship with the individuals parents will act as a disguise for the strained and complicated relationship that will exist behind closed doors. A position here can also suggest that the individual will be pleasant enough to their colleagues and supervisors at work while attempting to conceal their feelings of stress and dissatisfaction. The individual is likely to believe that they are in the heart of a maelstrom of office politics and this will make them very uncomfortable at work. The truth is however that they will be the cause of their own discomfort and that until they address their own emotions they will not be able to escape the situation.

If this configuration is found in the Hour Pillar, it suggests that the individual may be prone to making empty promises. The individual will not be assertive enough to decline a request and they will take on too much and find that they are unable to fulfil their commitments. They need to learn to be clear about their capacities and only take on the tasks they know they can complete or they will run the risk of losing the faith that their friends and colleagues had in them.

In the Luck Pillars, this configuration suggests that the individual will not be able to believe their own good luck. They will have achieved a great deal and they will have earned the respect of their colleagues but they will feel like a fraud and will consider themselves to be unworthy of this admiration. These people need to be careful that they don't start to sabotage their own success. They need to work on their self-esteem.

If this configuration is visible in the Annual Pillar, it is likely that promising deals will fall apart at the last minute. Throughout the course of the year, the indications will be that the individual's plans will be progressing smoothly but they may lose their nerve and start to worry at the closing stages. This anxiety may compel them to start going back over the details, making unnecessary alterations which cause all progress to be halted. They are advised to remain calm, keep a level head and avoid over-analysis.

Heaven Combine Earth Harm 天合地害
Xin Si 辛巳 (Metal Snake) + Bing Yin 丙寅 (Fire Tiger)

With the Heaven Combine Earth Harm configuration, the Heavenly Stem forms a Harm 害 with the Earthly Branch. Again it would seem that the outlook for this individual is very positive, but the Harm formation suggests hidden feelings. On this occasion, there is an undercurrent of insecurity and distrust.

An individual may encounter this Heaven Combine Earth Harm Pillar if it appears in their BaZi Natal Chart in either the Year, Month, or Hour Pillar, as well as the Luck Pillars, and the Annual Pillar.

If this configuration is found in the Year Pillar, it indicates insecurity with regard to their relationship with their grandparents. It could be that they feel they are unable to trust or relate with their grandparents. As the Year Pillar also represents one's social circle, this configuration denotes that the Xin Si does not have a close bond with his/her friends and doubts the sincerity of the friendship.

When found in the Month Pillar, this configuration indicates that these same emotions will instead have a bearing on the individual's relationship with their parents; possibly they will feel unable to confide in their parents. Alternatively, as the Month Pillar also governs work and career, they may be insecure about their working relationships and they may fear that a colleague will take credit for their ideas.

If this configuration is found in the Hour Pillar the individual may fear that their children are not being honest with them. They may also be struggling in their relationships with their employees, customers or suppliers. In addition, these individuals may feel unfulfilled in life as they are unable or find difficulty in realizing their goals.

Metal Snake

When this configuration is seen in the Luck Pillar, it is an indication that a period of apparent good fortune will end in a feeling of being victimized. The individual is likely to become very jaded and cynical about their work and employers. It is possible that work related stress has had a negative impact on their health or relationships and the individual doesn't believe that the emotional price they paid can ever be compensated.

In the Annual Pillar, this configuration suggests that a promising year will end in disappointments. The individual is recommended to look at their achievements without prejudice and think again. It is likely that they have achieved enough and they should be proud, but instead they have allowed jealousy to cloud their judgement and change their perceptions.

Heaven Friend Earth Clash 天比地冲
Xin Si 辛巳 (Metal Snake) + Xin Hai 辛亥 (Metal Pig)

Here the Xin Hai 辛亥 is forming the Heaven Friend Earth Clash with the Day Pillar. It indicates than an initial agreement will be unsettled by changes in circumstance and will eventually end in disagreement. People with this configuration in their Chart will be compelled to keep busy, they will always have a packed schedule but for all their activity they will fail to achieve anything.

This Pillar also suggests that promises may fail to live up to the anticipation. The individual is likely to feel very frustrated and disappointed that events have not followed the expected course. However, the unexpected isn't always a bad thing. The ultimate outcome will depend on the Heavenly Stem. If the Heavenly Stem is positive, even a negative turn of events may lead to something beneficial.

When this configuration appears in the Natal Chart these feelings and circumstances will impact upon the individual's relationships. When this configuration is found in the Year Pillar, the individual is likely to encounter some difficulties in their relationships with their grandparents following a change in circumstances. It could be that the individual discovers that they have to move away. The Year Pillar also represents a person's social circle and the configuration here could mean that this individual does not have strong friendships either because they are unable to connect well or conflict has marred the relationship.

If the configuration is in the Month Pillar, the individual may find that their relationship with their parents is confused and destabilised by a surprising event or revelation. As the Month Pillar also governs one's career, the individual's relationship with their employers may change after an announcement like a site move or a change in policy. Alternatively the individual may have an experience that radically alters their career goals and they may change their path altogether.

When this configuration is found in the Hour Pillar, the individual may fall to quarrelling with their children over some news or a change to their lives together. Alternatively their relationships with their customers may be altered in some unforeseen way. A position in the Hour Pillar, which is representative of a person's hopes and dreams, could also suggest that the individual may have their eyes opened to new ideas and new possibilities.

A Heaven Friend Earth Clash in the Luck Pillars is an indication of steady change. The individual is likely to have to endure through a long period of progression and growth. This may be a painful time but the individual should take comfort in the knowledge that the ultimate outcome will be a positive and they will understand why everything they went through was worthwhile.

When this configuration is found in the Annual Pillar, it indicates a year of surprise endings and unexpected outcomes. The individual will have to fight some private battles as they come to terms with the turmoil around them. Ultimately they will emerge enriched by self-discovery and experience.

Heaven and Earth Clash 天冲地冲
Xin Si 辛巳 (Metal Snake) + Ding Hai 丁亥 (Fire Pig)

This Heaven and Earth Clash Pillar is a configuration in which the Day Pillar is clashed by the Ding Hai 丁亥 Pillar. This is known as the Fan Yin 反吟 formation, an unlucky formation because it will have the effect of diminishing any of the good qualities of an individual's Day Pillar. In addition to reducing their abilities and making every achievement much harder to come by, this configuration may also act to put more barriers in the way.

Individuals in the Xin Si's circle who have this Pillar in their Chart may be a bad influence on the individual's career. They may be perfectly pleasant people, with very good intentions, but they may nevertheless be the source of poor advice.

Seen in the Natal Chart, this configuration indicates a lack of affinity with the individual or individuals represented by the specific Pillar in which it appears.

When seen in the Year Pillar, this configuration suggests that the individual will feel a lack of affinity with their grandparents. They may not be able to relate to their grandparents' old fashioned values or they may simply be unable to find the time to spend with them and get to know them. Alternatively the individual may feel quite misunderstood and find it quite difficult to make friends.

When this configuration is found in the Month Pillar, the individual may be unable to find a feeling of affinity with their parents. They may not be able to connect with them in any meaningful way as their opinions and motivations may be very disparate. Alternatively the individual may struggle to be noticed by their managers at work and their hard work may, as a result, go unrewarded.

Metal Snake

In the Hour Pillar, this configuration suggests that the individual does not have the relationship with their children that they may desire. It is possible that they have step children and they are finding it hard to build a strong bond with them. Equally they may be unable to develop a rapport with their key customers and clients and this may have a negative impact on their career.

Where this configuration is present in the Luck Pillar, the individual is likely to go through a very difficult and challenging time. There will be a lot of obstacles in their path and they may have to work their way through a series of setbacks. They are likely to feel much stressed at times and they will benefit from the support of their loved ones.

If this configuration occurs in the Annual Pillar, there may be a difficult year ahead and the individual is recommended to try and keep a low profile for the year. They should avoid making any serious decisions or significant changes where possible. They are also advised to refrain from making any major financial investments. Any new venture or relationship embarked on in this time is likely to end badly.

Heaven Counter Earth Clash 天剋地冲
Xin Si 辛巳 (Metal Snake) + Yi Hai 乙亥 (Wood Pig)

This Heaven Counter Earth Clash Pillar is a configuration the Day Pillar is going against the Yi Hai 乙亥. It is important to note that this configuration and the Heaven and Earth Clash formations are different. In this situation the Xin Si individual is in control. They will have passion and a strong desire to win. They are likely to be dominant characters with an entrepreneurial spirit who have tremendous potential to achieve great success but they must be careful not to be impatient or over hasty in their decision making.

An individual may encounter this Heaven Counter Earth Clash Pillar if it appears in their Natal Chart in either the Year, Month, or Hour Pillar, as well as the Luck Pillars, or the Annual Pillar.

When this configuration is seen in the Year Pillar, it suggests that the individual will be able to advance their career or improve the outlook for their business by seeking the support and guidance of high profile and well-connected friends.

It this configuration is found in the Month Pillar, the individual is likely to have a flair for business and a gift for turning a profit. They are likely to feel a thrill at the thought of making money but they should be wary of becoming avaricious and greedy.

In the Hour Pillar, this configuration is an indication that the individual will take dedication to their career to the extreme and that they will leave little time for their personal relationships. These individuals are advised to remember that money cannot buy happiness and that there is more to life than career success.

When found in the Luck Pillar, this configuration is an indication that the individual will be very driven with a strong business sense and an entrepreneurial spirit. They will be compelled to invest and pursue career success and material wealth. They are advised to keep a level head and to think clearly through their decisions.

When this configuration occurs in the Annual Pillar, the individual is likely to encounter a myriad of opportunities to generate and accumulate wealth throughout the year. They may begin a new venture or become involved in new partnerships. They may choose to invest in property. This may be a good time to start putting plans in place for the future. The individual is reminded to take just a little time to relax with their family as the year progresses as although it will be a fruitful, it will also be a stressful one.

Heaven and Earth Unity 天同地比
Xin Si 辛巳 (Metal Snake) + Xin Si 辛巳 (Metal Snake)

If you see another Xin Si in the Chart, this will form a Fu Yin 伏吟 configuration. This Heaven and Earth Unity denotes a sad emotional events which is why it is often referred to as the hidden warning Pillar.

An individual may encounter this Fu Yin formation if it appears in their BaZi Natal Chart in either the Year Pillar, the Month Pillar, or the Hour Pillar, the Luck Pillar or the Annual Pillar.

If the Heaven and Earth Unity is found in the Year Pillar, the individual is likely to have a difficult relationship with their grandparents. If their grandparents are still alive, the relationship is likely to be quite cold and emotionally distant. It is equally possible that they may never have met their grandparents.

In the Month Pillar, this configuration suggests that the individual will lack for the support of their parents. The relationship is likely to be quite strained, it may be characterised by arguments or by uncomfortable silence. There is also an indication that these individuals may find that they are unable to inherit, be it a property or a business.

When this configuration is found in the Hour Pillar, it suggests significant distance in the individual's relationship to children. It is possible that they may not have any children and that problems with fertility have made it hard or impossible, alternatively they may have children who live apart from them.

If this configuration is visible in the Luck Pillar, there are religious or spiritual implications. This individual is likely to take their religious views very seriously and they may even take up a religious calling. Alternatively it may be their health that dominates their lives and they may be very focused on making sure they eat the right diet and get enough exercise. Sadly, a position here may also indicate the loss of a parent.

In the Annual Pillar, this configuration suggests that the individual will benefit from a year of many achievements. They will see career progression and an increase in wealth and property. However behind their successes there will be at least one distressing event that will cast a shadow over the year.

Metal Snake

Heaven and Earth Combine 天地相合
Xin Si 辛巳 (Metal Snake) + Bing Shen 丙申 (Fire Monkey)

The Heaven and Earth Combine is the most desirable of the Pillars. It is an indication that the individual will be able to relate easily to others and that they will be able to build strong relationships and positive connections that will help them to achieve their personal and professional goals. This configuration is often thought to be a predictor of happiness.

This Pillar will even have a positive effect on the Xin Si if appears in the Chart of someone in their circle. Anyone with this configuration in their chart is likely to be a good friend and a good influence.

An individual may encounter this Heaven and Earth Combine Pillar if it appears in their BaZi Natal Chart in either the Year, Month, or Hour Pillars, as well as the Luck Pillars, and the Annual Pillar.

If this configuration is seen in the Year Pillar, the individual is likely to enjoy the warmth and support of their grandparents and friends. As the Year Pillar represents a person's social circle, the configuration here means that they are also likely to be very popular with a good social standing that will help them to open doors and gain influence.

When this configuration is seen in the Month Pillar, the individual is likely to be very close to their parents. They will appreciate the comfort and council that their parents are able to offer in times of need. The Month Pillar also governs one's work and career. This indicates that they are also likely to find it easy to be noticed and have their voices heard in their places of work as they will have the respect and professional regard of their managers and colleagues.

When this configuration is found in the Hour Pillar, the individual will enjoy a loving and affectionate relationship with their children. Their homes will be filled with light and laughter. They are also likely to be able to build an easy rapport with their clients and customers and will be able to depend upon their loyalty. The Hour Pillar also represents one's hopes and dreams, so the configuration here would reflect their likelihood of achieving their goals in life without much difficulty.

If this configuration is present in either the Luck or Annual Pillars, the individual will be happy in love and marriage and have the confidence and security that only a firm familial foundation can provide. They are also likely to find career success through joint ventures, partnerships and cooperation.

Rob Wealth Goat Blade 劫財羊刃
Xin Si 辛巳 (Metal Snake) + Geng Xu 庚戌 (Metal Dog)

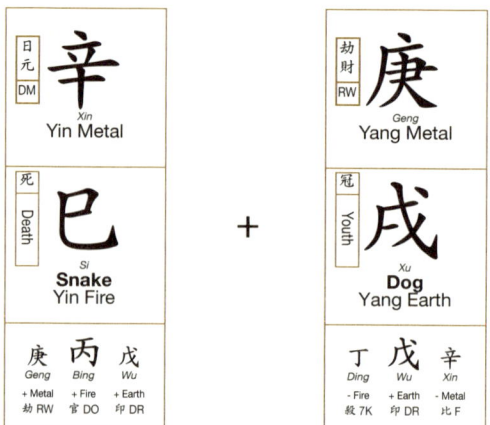

If you are a Xin Si, you do not want to see a Geng Xu 庚戌 Pillar in your Chart. This will form a Rob Wealth Goat Blade 劫財羊刃 formation, which is an indication of serious financial loss and emotional or relationship problems. Individuals who have this configuration in their Chart may find their goals hard to achieve and that they fail to accomplish as much as they had hoped. They are likely to be left feeling disappointed and demoralized.

Anyone connected to the Xin Si with this Pillar in their Chart may prove to be a cause of them losing money. It is not that they will try to con them or to take the money from them and in fact it is unlikely that either party will be aware that it's happening until much later, if they ever find out at all. These people may be very good friends and it is possible that they may be found to have been the unwitting source of poor financial advice. Alternatively it may be that the two of them have a tendency to be rather extravagant and to overspend when they are together.

辛未

Xin Wei

| 辛丑 | 辛卯 | 辛巳 | 辛未 | 辛酉 | 辛亥 |
| Xin Chou | Xin Mao | Xin Si | Xin Wei | Xin You | Xin Hai |

Getting to Know
Xin Wei 辛未 (Metal Goat)

Xin Wei

Positive Imagery

Negative Imagery

Getting to Know
Xin Wei 辛未 (Metal Goat)

General Observations:

Buried treasure that is dirty and dull is representative of the Xin Wei Pillar. This reflects individuals that may appear unrefined or unattractive on the surface, but deep inside hides more substance to their character.

Xin Wei 辛未 individuals are charming, friendly and popular. Their natural leadership qualities push them to be independent and enable them to achieve great personal success. What they ultimately want is fame and power, and enjoy the competition involved in order to gain it.

Individuals born under this Pillar are shrewd, and able to quickly assess people and situations. This is why when they are in positions of authority, they tend to be vigorous and forceful. They have a domineering and take-charge personality, and have little tolerance for error. Others see this and revere it.

Their self-confidence points them towards unique enterprising opportunities. They are able to apply their full attention on one goal, which is why the opportunities they choose turn out to be a success.

Travel and freedom are very important to the Xin Wei as well. They are so essential, that they often will tailor their careers around it. Their love for freedom also plays a major role in their deep need for self-expression.

If their need for power is not channelled properly, they will become manipulative. They have a deeply conniving personality and will not hesitate to backstab others who they feel are in their way. Learning the art of compromise will go a long way in avoiding this.

When it comes to material things, the Xin Wei can be frivolous. If they are not watchful, they will fall into periods of extravagance or self-indulgence. They usually are not left with an inheritance. For this reason, they have no support to fall back on. It is best that they invest and save their money wisely.

Creating order in their lives helps them to avoid impulsive action. Avoiding reckless actions can cease them from fluctuating in their financial circumstances and also help them to make the best long term financial decisions.

Deep within, the Xin Wei may experience insecurities about whether they are making the right decisions. By focusing on their true purpose, they will be able to always make the proper choices and gain wisdom in the process. Another way to eradicate insecurities is by developing their humanitarian side. This will help them to stop worrying.

Compared to other Xin Metals, the Xin Wei are considered dull and drab in appearance. They often look unrefined and unappealing, which may be the source of their inherent issues with self-image. They are often highly self-conscious.

In addition to being somewhat unattractive, they are also plagued with serious illnesses that last throughout their life time. As they get older, their issues may subside, however, they may encounter problems with their feet.

Metal Goat

Key Character Traits of the Xin Wei 辛未: Overall

- Witty
- Good communicator
- Innovative
- Cunning
- Seeking Power
- Impatient
- A Natural Leader
- Intuitive
- Vain
- Tactful

Work Life

Xin Wei

Professional Self

There are two factors that are highly important for the Xin Wei when pursuing their careers: financial reward and freedom to travel. Any career that they pursue must provide them with financial benefits and changes in routine.

They are ambitious, which is why they need a career that offers variety and spunk. When they are in a position that offers variety, they are able to explore new ideas. Once the Xin Wei are excited about what they are doing, they will propel instantly towards success.

With strong organizational skills and a charming personality, they make good leaders and are able to inspire others with their ideas and concepts. Coupled this with their steadfast determination, they are likely to thrive in the business world.

Through education, they are essentially a perfect fit for any profession.

Career Options

Many career options are available to the Xin Wei. By successfully channelling their abilities, they will be able to seize success in any area.

Careers that allow them to express their individuality are best. Ideal careers for them in this area include photography, art, writing, journalism, music, or entertainment. They are likely to find substantial success in these fields.

Metal Goat

Alternatively, the Xin Wei may want to use their analytical skills in vocations such as science, technology or law.

For those who want to deal in the public sector, they should choose careers in politics, media, teaching, or psychology. Occupations in religion and metaphysics are also possible due to their interest in spirituality.

Because they have such a strong desire to succeed, nearly any area they pursue would provide them with growth and success.

Key Character Traits of the Xin Wei 辛未: Work life

Positive

- Considerate
- Responsible
- Intuitive
- Hardworking
- Versatile
- Protective

Negative

- Opinionated
- Domineering
- Selfish
- Crafty
- Impatient
- Insecure

Love and Relationships

Xin
Wei

Love

Xin Wei individuals are charming, which is what attracts others to them. As partners, they are very protective and will do anything for that special someone in their life.

Xin Wei individuals look for relationships with people who share their interests. They have a deep appreciation of wisdom and are attracted to others who value the same. Those who are great communicators are also appealing to them.

Most often, these individuals want to keep the peace in their relationships. However, they are prone to moodiness and this can interfere with their desire for peace.

If they really want their relationships to work, the Xin Wei should be careful not to become bossy or critical of their partners.

Acquaintances

As friends, the Xin Wei are supportive and understanding. When they are in large social settings, they are lively and fun to be around.

The healthiest friendships for the Xin Wei are those that provide mental stimulation. They prefer the company of others who are clever, compelling and interesting. They are highly emotional and have a strong need for connections. Once they establish a bond, they will always keep their allies near.

Metal Goat

They are so conscious of their image that they worry about what their friends think of them. In the midst of guarding their self-image, they need to watch out for appearing too arrogant or conceited.

Family

Home and family life are highly important to the Xin Wei. Home life is important because that is where they feel most secure. They are dedicated and will go above and beyond for the well-being of their family.

Another reason they value home life so is due to the strong male figure from their early years. This influence creates a somewhat old fashioned idea of what family dynamics are all about.

Marriage is a good decision for the Xin Wei. They are willing to form long lasting and stable relationships with their partner. However, early marriage is not the best idea for them. It is best that they take their time before settling down. It allows them enough space to mature and prepares them for the responsibilities of love and marriage.

Ultimately, their spousal relationships will be good and they will produce many children.

Key Character Traits of the Xin Wei 辛未: Love & Relationships

- Although ambitious, there is a need for relationship security
- High value for friendship
- Later life marriage are more auspicious
- Large families
- Attracted to strong minds
- Potential for insecurity

Metal Goat

Famous Personalities

Evgeny "Eugene" Shvidler - Russian oil businessman. He is also the chairman of Millhouse, LLC, an investment and asset management firm.

Gordon Ramsay - British chef, restaurateur and television personality. He has been awarded fifteen Michelin stars so far in his career. He is a perfectionist infamously known for his fiery temper and use of profanities.

Richard Li Tzar Kai - Hong Kong businessman and philanthropist. He is the youngest son of the eighth richest man in the world (2013), Li Ka-Shing.

Source: Wikipedia (June 2013)

Technical Analysis

Xin
Wei

BaZi Day Pillar Analytics 日柱分析

時 Hour	日 Day	月 Month	年 Year	
	辛 **Xin** Yin Metal [日元 DM]			Heavenly Stems 天干
	未 **Wei** Goat Yin Earth [衰 Weakening]			Earthly Branches 地支
	乙 Yi - Wood 才 IW / 己 Ji - Earth 卩 IR / 丁 Ding - Fire 殺 7K			Hidden Stems 藏干

Description

This Xin Wei 辛未 is an auspicious Pillar that has the Wood Storage 庫, and is supported by the Resource element. There are indications of great fortune in life as this Pillar sits on the Indirect Wealth 偏財星, Indirect Resource 偏印星 and Seven Killings 七殺星 Stars.

The Xin Wei individual has a need to achieve. They are hardworking and determined and they are capable of taking on a tremendous amount of responsibility. However they are also imaginative and creative with a love of travel and exploration. They may sometimes feel conflicted by these two desires.

The Xin Wei individual is very ambitious, an attribute of the hidden Seven Killings Star 七殺星. Financial security is important to them and they will use material wealth as a bench mark for their successes in life. They are analytical, highly intelligent and willing to do whatever it takes to turn an idea into a tangible reality. Their strong values and good judgement combined with their business sense and executive abilities should give them the skills they need to attain everything they wish for. It may benefit them to create a plan of action and stick to it regardless of challenges and discouragement.

At their best the Xin Wei individual is charming and gracious (courtesy of the Indirect Resource Star 偏印星). They are very intuitive and are capable of making the best out of any situation. They have an instinctive understanding of group dynamics and of the feelings, needs and motivations of those around them. They enjoy group activities which allow them to learn from others and they will be very helpful and friendly. At times, however, the Xin Wei individual can lose contact with their insight and become lost in their own needs and sensitivities.

The Xin Wei can be confident to the point of arrogance. Their stubbornness may make them domineering and it is possible for them to be quite selfish, unreasonable and manipulative. These are the combined effects of the Indirect Wealth and Seven Killings Stars. They can be very critical and even judgemental of the people around them, allowing their opinions to be driven by their moods and feelings. This extreme behaviour can often be a manifestation of their profound emotional insecurities which they may find it hard to discuss. The Xin Wei individual is very sensitive, they are easily discouraged by criticism and they have a deep need for stability. This need is so intense that they often struggle with change and this can make them controlling and inflexible. They must work hard to reconcile these extremes of confidence and vulnerability in order to develop a more balanced view and develop genuine faith in their abilities.

The Xin Wei craves love and attention. They appreciate a harmonious atmosphere and they will want to develop a firm foundation for themselves and their families. In the home they will want to be in control and they will be the voice of authority regardless of gender. They may need to learn to let go a little in order to not overwhelm their loved ones.

Metal Goat

Technical Observations

Since the Xin Wei 辛未 represents a Metal element grown from the Earth, it is considered to be less pure and brilliant in comparison to the other Xin Metal Pillars. The Xin Wei will rely on the quality of the Earth elements in their Chart for prosperity and longevity and it is most favourable for them if they have the support of the Wu 戊 and Ji 己.

The positive presence of the Ren 壬 and Gui 癸 Water elements is also essential, as this will help to cleanse the Qi. The individual's achievements in life and their overall reputation will depend greatly on the presence of Water element. Without the Water element, the Xin Wei individual will become stubborn and gullible. He or she will not able to achieve any significant success in life. Therefore, it is important that both Water and Earth elements are not harmed in the Chart.

A meeting with excessive Jia 甲 or Yi 乙 should, where possible, be avoided as the Wood element counters the ever-important Earth element. This Pillar will also come into difficulties with the Yin Hour 陰時 because the Xin Wei may not be able to deploy their Indirect Resource Star 偏印星 as their sixth sense. Yin Hour refers to the hours before sunrise. It will render their sixth sense or intuition inaccurate.

A Xin Wei person born in the Spring or Summer months may find that they face more obstacles and challenges than their peers, and this is likely to continue until they reach middle age. An individual born in the Autumn or Winter will be blessed with longevity. If their birthday falls in the Chen 辰 (Dragon) month, they may not experience the best of luck and they may have to work very hard for their success.

Unique 60 Pillar Combinations

This section covers the relationships between the individual pillar under this elemental polarity and several other pillars found in the 60 Jia Zi cycle.

Xin
Wei

Heaven Combine Earth Punish 天合地刑
Xin Wei 辛未 (Metal Goat) + Bing Xu 丙戌 (Fire Dog)

The Bing Xu 丙戌 will form the Heaven Combine Earth Punish configuration with the Day Pillar.

Often the appearance of the Heavenly Stem is considered to be an indication of a positive outlook, but as the Earthly Branch forms a Punishment there is instead an implication of tension, emotional pain, and stress. This suggests an external appearance of happiness that will act as a disguise for the pain and negativity that is hidden underneath.

An individual may encounter this Heaven Combine Earth Punish Pillar if is appears in their Natal Chart in either the Year, Month, or Hour Pillars, the Luck Pillars, or the Annual Pillar.

When this configuration is seen in the Year Pillar, it indicates that an outwardly favourable relationship with the individual's grandparents will be little more than a veneer for the tension and unhappiness that will truly characterise the relationship.

If this configuration is found in the Month Pillar, the indications will be the same only this time with reference to the individual's parents. A position here will also have a bearing on the individual's career and it could be that though they will smile and be cordial with their colleagues they will not feel at all comfortable in the workplace. They will be consumed by fears over boardroom politics and they will be convinced that the atmosphere is rife with tension. They may need to take a closer look at their feelings and ask themselves what evidence they have for their convictions. It is likely that they will be the victim of their own suspicious minds and they may need to learn to let go and have faith in their colleagues.

In the Hour Pillar, this configuration indicates that the individual may have a tendency to make empty promises. They may be too concerned about hurting people's feelings to feel comfortable enough to decline a task, even when they know they don't have enough room in their schedule to take it on. They need to learn that they will cause more disappointment if they fail to fulfil a commitment than they would do if they were simply to decline in the first instance. If they don't become more assertive they may find that they lose the faith their friends and colleagues had in them.

Metal Goat

When this configuration is present in the Luck Pillars, the indications are actually very positive from the outside. The individual is likely to achieve a great deal and will be well on their way to accomplishing their goals. They will have the respect and admiration of their friends and colleagues. Inside, however, the individual will feel unworthy and their insecurity and uncertainty may lead them to sabotage their own progress. The advice here is that the individual needs to learn to see in themselves all the talent and potential that everyone else knows it there. It is vital that they work on their self-esteem.

In the Annual Pillar, this configuration indicates a year in which many promising arrangements may be postponed or cancelled at the last minute. The individual is advised to try to remain calm through the year and not allow their fears to get the better of them. This may not be easy as there is likely to be a lot of tension and distrust in the work place but it will be important as it will, almost certainly, be the individual's own last minute worries, and the resulting alterations, that causes their plans to be derailed.

Heaven Combine Earth Harm 天合地害
Xin Wei 辛未 (Metal Goat) + Bing Zi 丙子 (Fire Rat)

The Bing Zi will form the Heaven Combine Earth Harm Pillar with the Day Pillar. Again this would appear to indicate that the outlook is very positive, but under the surface the individual will have concerns about their relationships and they may even fear for the loyalty of their loved ones.

If this configuration is found in the Year Pillar, the impact will be felt in the individual's relationship with their grandparents and friends. It could be that they feel they are unable to be completely open with their grandparents or that their friends might betray their secrets.

When found in the Month Pillar, this configuration indicates that these same emotions will instead have a bearing on the individual's relationship with their parents; possibly they will feel unable to confide in their parents.

Alternatively they may be insecure about their working relationships and they may fear that a colleague will take credit for their ideas.

If this configuration is found in the Hour Pillar the individual may fear that their children are not being honest with them. They may also be struggling in their relationships with their employees, customers or suppliers. Possibly they are concerned that their suppliers are overcharging them or providing them with sub-standard materials.

In the Luck Pillars, this configuration denotes a situation in which the individual may appear to achieve a tremendous amount but rather than feeling proud, they find that they are feeling abused or victimised. They are obviously going to feel very disappointed that all their hard work has led to such an unhappy conclusion. They are likely to be very cynical about their work and colleagues.

When found in the Annual Pillar, this configuration indicates a very promising year that ends in disappointment. It is likely that the individual has allowed an unfavourable comparison to the achievements of another to alter their perception of their own accomplishments. They need to be wary of allowing jealousy to discourage them. They have succeeded in all they set out to do and they need to accept that that is enough.

Heaven Friend Earth Clash 天比地冲
Xin Wei 辛未 (Metal Goat) + Xin Chou 辛丑 (Metal Ox)

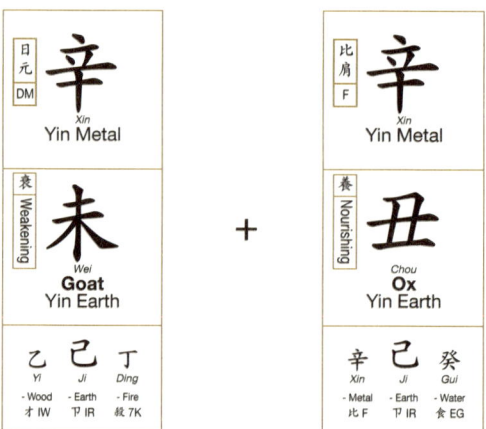

The Heaven Friend Earth Clash Pillar denotes a situation in which an agreement at the outset is pulled apart by changes in circumstance. People with this Pillar in their chart may often find that they are very busy, they work hard and are always active but they may fail to achieve anything of substance with all their efforts. Combined, these effects indicate that events will not follow the anticipated course. The individual is likely to feel unsettled and disappointed but they may do well to remember that the unexpected is not always a bad thing. If the element of the Heavenly Stem is favourable there will be a positive conclusion to the chaos. Even an apparently negative turn of events will ultimately prove to have beneficial effects.

When this configuration appears in the Natal Chart in the Year, Month or Hour Pillars it will have an impact on the individual's relationships.

If this configuration is found in the Year Pillar, there will unexpected events and surprises in connection with or resulting from the individual's relationships with their grandparents and friends.

In the Month Pillar, the indications will be the same with regard to the authority figures in the individual's life. They are likely to be confused or disappointed by unforeseen circumstances that throw their relationship with their parents off balance. Alternatively their career path may take an unanticipated turn; possibly they will be made redundant or asked to work overseas.

When seen in the Hour Pillar, this configuration could indicate a change in the individual's relationship with their children or with their employees, clients and suppliers. Alternatively they may experience a sudden epiphany and radically change their views on the world or they may find that they ideas they had been working lead in unexpected directions.

In the Luck Pillar, a Heaven Friend Earth Clash Pillar suggests that the individual will experience a decade of steady and continual change. The individual may face some painful and challenging situations which will alter their perceptions. This is a period of growth and progress and though it may be a difficult time it will lead to a positive conclusion.

If this configuration is seen in the Annual Pillar, it is an indication that the year will be full of surprises and unexpected twists and turns. The individual may need to take time to reassess and to think through the impact on their emotions and perspectives. They are likely to face some personal struggles as they reconcile all the new information but they will emerge enriched by the experience.

Heaven and Earth Clash 天冲地冲
Xin Wei 辛未 (Metal Goat) + Ding Chou 丁丑 (Fire Ox)

This Heaven and Earth Clash Pillar is a configuration in which the Day Pillar is clashed by the Ding Chou 丁丑 Pillar. This is known as the Fan Yin 反吟 formation and it is an unlucky formation because it will act to diminish any of the good qualities of an individual's Day Pillar. This configuration could have the additional effect of placing more barriers in the Xin Wei's path that, with their reduced abilities, they may find they are ill-equipped to surmount.

Anyone connected to the Xin Wei with this Pillar in their Chart will probably have a negative impact on their career. It is possible that they will be the source of poor advice however well-meaning that advice may have been.

Seen in the Natal Chart, this configuration indicates a lack of affinity with the individual or individuals represented by the specific Pillar in which it appears.

When seen in the Year Pillar, this configuration suggests that the individual will lack for a feeling of affinity with their grandparents. The relationship may be quite cold and formal and there will be little genuine affection there.

The Year Pillar also governs a person's social circle. This configuration here could mean that the individual may be quite shy and socially awkward, or does not have a close relationship with his/her friends.

When this configuration is found in the Month Pillar, the individual is likely to feel that they lack for an affinity with their parents. It may be that their parents disapprove of their priorities or of the path they chose in life. A position here may also connect to the individual's career, as the Month Pillar also represents one's work life. This could be an indication that they are struggling to find work or that they are not fully inspired and motivated by their profession.

In the Hour Pillar, this configuration points to a lack of affinity with children or employees. It could be that the individual has step-children that they are unable to build a connection with. They may also feel that they are unable to understand the needs and motivations of their workforce, customers or suppliers and are unable to build a rapport as a result. As the Hour Pillar governs one's ideas and hopes, it is equally possible that they will feel they are not making an adequate contribution to society or that they have lost step with their sense of purpose altogether.

Where this configuration is present in the Luck Pillar, the individual is likely to live through a very difficult decade. There will be challenges and obstacles at every turn and their goals may seem to be unachievable. This is not a positive Pillar and the individual may benefit from the support and comfort of their friends.

In the Annual Pillar, this configuration is an indication that the individual is likely to find that they do not enjoy the best of luck during the year. It is recommended that they keep a low profile and they should avoid making any major decisions or significant changes where possible. The indications are that any new investment, venture or relationship, commenced at this time, will more than likely end badly.

Heaven Counter Earth Clash 天剋地冲
Xin Wei 辛未 (Metal Goat) + Yi Chou 乙丑 (Wood Ox)

This Heaven Counter Earth Clash Pillar is a configuration in which the Day Pillar is going against the Yi Chou 乙丑. It is important to note that this configuration and the Heaven and Earth Clash formations are different. In this situation the Xin Wei is empowered and given a need to control. They will have passion and a strong desire to win. They are likely to be dominant characters, with an entrepreneurial spirit, who have a great deal of potential to achieve success but they must be careful not to be impatient or over hasty in their decision making.

An individual may encounter this Heaven Counter Earth Clash Pillar if it appears in their Natal Chart in either the Year, Month, or Hour Pillar, as well as the Luck Pillars, or the Annual Pillar.

When this configuration is seen in the Year Pillar, it suggests that the individual will be able to better promote their skills and their businesses through the assistance of high-profile friends. These people will be able to advise them

on the direction they should take and they could provide invaluable information and networking opportunities.

It this configuration is found in the Month Pillar, the individual is likely to be business minded with a gift for finance. They will almost certainly have the ability to build up their material wealth very quickly and they may find the process thrilling but they would be well advised to guard against allowing their ambition to turn into avarice and greed.

Metal Goat

In the Hour Pillar, this configuration indicates that the individual is likely to take their dedication to their career to the point of an obsession. They will almost certainly be a workaholic. These individuals may do well to be reminded not to forget that they have a responsibility to their families as well as their careers and that true happiness requires more than career success.

When found in the Luck Pillar, this configuration suggests that the individual will have the skills and the opportunity to become very wealthy. They are likely to have a good eye for an investment and an entrepreneurial flair. They would be wise to make the most of a decade of good fortune but they should be careful not to rush their decisions.

When this configuration occurs in the Annual Pillar, the individual is likely to encounter a myriad of opportunities to generate and accumulate wealth throughout the year. They may invest in property or become involved in new ventures and new working partnerships. While the individual is advised to work hard to get the greatest benefit out of this time, they are also advised that though the year will be fruitful, it will also be stressful. They should know that their family and their health might show the strain of their long working hours, and it might be wise to spare just a little time to relax.

Heaven and Earth Unity 天同地比
Xin Wei 辛未 (Metal Goat) + Xin Wei 辛未 (Metal Goat)

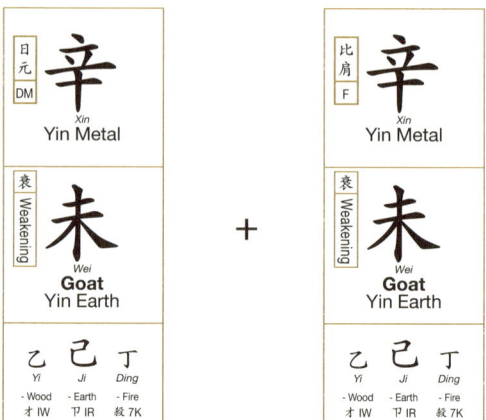

If you see another Xin Wei in the Chart, this forms a Fu Yin 伏吟 formation. This Heaven and Earth Unity formation is an indication of sorrow and events that deal an emotional impact. For this reason, it is often referred to as the hidden warning Pillar.

An individual may encounter this Fu Yin formation if it appears in their BaZi Natal Chart in either the Year Pillar, the Month Pillar, or the Hour Pillar, the Luck Pillar or the Annual Pillar.

If this configuration appears in the Year Pillar, the individual is likely to feel a lack of affinity with their grandparents. It may be that the relationship is a very weak one or it could even be that the individual has never met their grandparents before. As the Year Pillar governs one's social circle, this configuration would mean that the individual may feel detached or even lonely despite having many friends. It is possible that these friends are not close with the individual or that they do not have a strong bond. Therefore, this individual is unable to rely or trust them.

When seen in the Month Pillar, this configuration suggests that the individual will lack affinity with their parents. They may struggle to be able to connect on any profound level, and it is possible that they may not even be on speaking terms with one or both parents. This could result from, or lead to, an inability to take on the family business. There is also an indication that the parents may be unwilling or unable to pass on an inheritance. The individual may also find it hard to advance in their career as they are unable to find support from their superiors or peers. This is because the Month Pillar also governs one's work life and career prospects.

If this configuration is found in the Hour Pillar, the individual will experience a significant lack of affinity with children. They may have been separated from their children, who are being brought up by their grandparents or a previous partner. It is also possible that the individual may not have children and, though they may profoundly wish to bring life into the word, they may find that they are challenged. They may also face difficulty in achieve their goals in life as the Hour Pillar represents a person's hopes and dreams.

In the Luck Pillar, this configuration points to a spiritual path as this is very often thought to be the spiritual Pillar. It is likely that the individual will become very religious and they may even choose to take up a religious vocation. They may equally become very focused on their health and develop an obsession with their diet and exercise. There is also a sad indication of the potential to lose a parent.

If this configuration is visible in the Annual Pillar, the individual is likely to have a very successful year in terms of career progression. They may also see an increase in property or wealth, but behind these achievements, there will be at least one emotionally straining event.

Heaven and Earth Combine 天地相合
Xin Wei 辛未 (Metal Goat) + Bing Wu 丙午 (Fire Horse)

The Heaven and Earth Combine is the most desirable Pillar to be seen in the BaZi Chart. This Pillar is often thought to be a predictor of success and happiness. Individuals with this Pillar in their Chart will be blessed with the ability to develop a positive affinity with the people they meet leading to strong connections and warm relationships.

If this configuration is found in the BaZi Chart of anyone connected to the Xin Wei, it is likely that these individuals will enjoy a special affinity with them. They will prove to be very helpful and to have a positive influence.

An individual may encounter this Heaven and Earth Combine Pillar if it appears in their Natal Chart in either the Year, Month, or Hour Pillars, the Luck Pillars, or the Annual Pillar.

If this configuration is found in the Year Pillar, it suggests that the individual will have a warm and pleasant relationship with their grandparents or friends. They will never lack for a place to go when they are in need of comfort. They are also likely to be very popular, with a good social status which will allow them to be introduced into the right circles and to make the right contacts to best benefit their progression.

In the Month Pillar, this configuration suggests that the individual will have an excellent relationship with their parents. They will be able to go to their parents for advice and support. They are also likely to have a positive working relationship with their managers and colleagues. They will be respected and admired.

If this configuration is found in the Hour Pillar, the individual will be a good parent. They will have a loving and trusting relationship with their children and they will always be proud of them. They are also likely to be very successful in their careers as their positive relationships with their suppliers and customers will allow them to broker the best deals and deliver the most competitive service.

If this configuration is found in the Luck Pillars or Annual Pillar, it is an indication that the individual will be personally happy and professionally successful. They will be lucky in love and supported by loyal friends and family. They would be wise to become involved in working partnerships and joint ventures as it is likely that through these they will see the greatest benefit to their careers.

Rob Wealth Goat Blade 劫财羊刃
Xin Wei 辛未 (Metal Goat) + Geng Xu 庚戌 (Metal Dog)

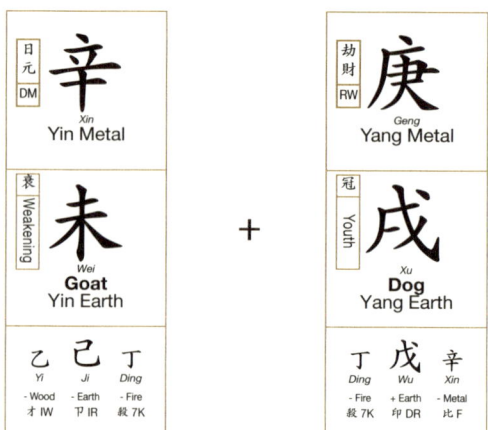

If you are a Xin Wei, you do not want to see a Geng Xu 庚戌 Pillar in your Chart. This will form a Rob Wealth Goat Blade 劫财羊刃 formation, which is an indication of serious financial losses and emotional or relationship problems. People who have this configuration in their Chart may find that they are drained and exhausted by hard work that appears to lead nowhere.

The Xin Wei individual should also be aware that anyone with this Pillar in their Chart may cause them to lose money. It is not that these people will try and take money from them; it is likely that neither party will be aware of what is happening at the time. It is possible that they may simply be a catalyst for the Xin Wei to overspend.

辛酉

Xin You

辛丑	辛卯	辛巳	辛未	辛酉	辛亥
Xin Chou	Xin Mao	Xin Si	Xin Wei	Xin You	Xin Hai

Getting to Know

Xin You 辛酉 (Metal Rooster)

Negative Imagery

辛酉
Metal Rooster

Getting to Know
Xin You 辛酉 (Metal Rooster)

General Observations:

The visual representation for the Xin You 辛酉 Pillar is the pointy blades of scissors or knives, or eye-catching glistening jewellery. It reflects the Xin You individuals that are a unique combination of beauty and brains. Not only are they attractive, they are also astute and sharp. Xin You individuals are furthermore, charismatic, charming, and persuasive. Xin You individuals have a great sense of humour too. They are respected and admired for their power and are often seen as true visionaries.

Spontaneity and impulse keep the Xin You's life full of action. They are not afraid of taking risks. In fact, taking risks is what makes them happiest. For them, time is of the essence. Because of this, they aim to seize all of life's opportunities. By constantly seizing life's opportunities, they can transform even the most hopeless situation into a success story.

These individuals are intuitive, inventive, and original. Once they allow their creative spirit to flow, they feel most fulfilled. Xin You women are also more likely to be broad minded and virtuous than men of the same Pillar.

These individuals are able to easily attract money and have great instincts regarding finances. However, it is important that they learn how to budget and make long term investments in order to keep their finances intact.

When it comes to difficult situations, they have no trouble facing them head on. They are true fighters and will do whatever is necessary in order to reach the top. They must however, be willing to take constructive criticism in order to improve themselves and avoid mistakes. Often times, instead of taking constructive criticism, they become oversensitive and defensive. As a result, they tend to not absorb and utilize their critiques.

They need a strong foundation, and should be wary of dispersing their energies into too many directions. By listening to their intuition and effectively applying their hard work, they can improve their life and increase their success.

Key Character Traits of the Xin You 辛酉: Overall

- Good at Communicating
- Successful
- Sharp
- Hard working
- Attractive
- Loves taking risk
- Financially motivated
- Good business acumen

Work Life

Xin You

Professional Self

Due to their intellect, and discipline, they are bound to be successful in any career path that they choose. For them, nothing defines success better than paving their own career path. It is highly important then that they choose a career that allots them freedom.

They have innate leadership skills and will easily rise in positions of authority because of their dynamic personality.

Their areas of strength are in business, art, teaching, and finances. These are the career sectors that they will easily rise to the top in.

Career Options

There is a never ending list of good career options for Xin You individuals. With so many skills and talents, they would fit right in with just about any profession.

Their persuasive nature along with their people skills would make them great promoters, television presenters and salesman. These same traits would also make them a great fit for positions in public relations and management.

If they would like to put their systematic thinking skills to good use, they may find interest in science, or engineering career fields.

Some Xin You's may prefer to use their artistic nature. In these cases, they would fit well in career fields relating to the arts, writing, speaking, singing or anything involving entertainment.

In addition, these individuals have a humanitarian streak and would therefore find happiness in careers connected to healing or charity.

Metal Rooster

Metal Rooster

Key Character Traits of the Xin You 辛酉: Work life

Positive

- Creative
- Funny
- Disciplined
- Optimistic
- Competitive
- Responsible
- Independent
- Leader

Negative

- Overbearing
- Egotistical
- Impatient
- Restless
- Power-Hungry
- Stubborn
- Lack of Self-Esteem

Love and Relationships

Xin You

Metal Rooster

Love

The Xin You are witty and entertaining, which is why they have no trouble finding admirers. However, there are certain qualities that potential suitors of the Xin You must meet.

First, their admirers must be clever and mentally stimulating. Mental stimulation is important because it keeps the Xin You sharp and on their toes.

Next, these individuals need someone who is reliable and supportive. This helps to ensure a pleasant environment and loving home.

Furthermore, their potential suitors should be successful, powerful and accomplished. This ensures that both partners are equal.

With requirements like these, it makes it difficult for anyone to live up to their high expectations.
However, it is important because they will often lose interest if their partner is not ambitious or intelligent.

Acquaintances

Xin You individuals make excellent friends. They are charming, gregarious and actively social.

Although they are highly social, they take their friendships seriously and desire to gain genuine friends. For this purpose, they will seek out friends who possess the same hardworking and intellectual traits as they do.

These individuals tend to attract all types of people into their lives. They need to be more discriminating with who they choose as friends. This will prevent them from wasting their time on those who do not have their best interest at heart.

Metal Rooster

Family

These individuals are home and family oriented, therefore, family life is favourable for the Xin You. Their ambition and determination plays a large role in their family life. They want the best for their family and will work to ensure it. This is one of many reasons why their family look to them for support and guidance.

Their marriages are favourable. They enjoy a partner who understands them fully and who supports them in all circumstances.

Unexpected events may occur in the marriage that will overshadow their joy. If they allow it, it will bring sorrow and unhappiness.

Metal Rooster

Key Character Traits of the Xin You 辛酉: Love & Relationships

- Attracted to smart and powerful people
- A good host/ess
- Potential difficulties in marriage
- Tendency to lose interest
- High partnership expectations
- Prone to changes of the heart

Famous Personalities

David Letterman - American television host and comedian. He has been a talk show host since 1980, and is currently hosting the popular late night talk show, *Late Show with David Letterman*.

Anwar Ibrahim - Malaysian politician and leader of the Opposition (Pakatan Rakyat) of Malaysia. He was the 7th Deputy Prime Minister of Malaysia.

Marilyn Monroe - American actress, singer, model, cultural icon and sex symbol. She was married and divorced three times. She died in 1962 at the age of 36 from an overdose, which was classified as "probable suicide".

Matt Damon - American award-winning actor, screenwriter, producer and philanthropist. He is one of the top 40 highest-grossing actors of all time.

Source: Wikipedia (June 2013)

Technical Analysis

Xin You

BaZi Day Pillar Analytics 日柱分析

時 Hour	日 Day	月 Month	年 Year	
	辛 Xin Yin Metal (DM)			天干 Heavenly Stems
	酉 You Rooster Yin Metal (祿 Thriving)			地支 Earthly Branches
	辛 Xin - Metal 比 F			藏干 Hidden Stems

Metal Rooster

Description

This Xin 辛 Metal is seated on the Thriving Star 祿星 and is Rooted 通根 in the Branch. This suggests that these individuals are highly intelligent and capable in their chosen field. They have a gift for the written word and literature. Xin You individuals need very little help and support from others to achieve this.

Xin You individuals are true originals. The Friend Star 比肩星 inside the You 酉 (Rooster) makes them witty, sharp, funny and attractive. It matters not a bit to them if their thoughts and opinions seem outlandish to others. They are independent and innovative, courageous and pioneering with a drive to explore the world and strike out on their own. They have a natural aesthetic sense and sharp mind; there are few tasks that would be beyond their capability.

The Xin You often reaches the very top of their profession, especially if it primarily involves speaking and talking. They are hardworking and intelligent with strong analytical skills and ingenious problem solving abilities. They are likely to seek a solid grounding in education and so they will, almost certainly, be knowledgeable and they have plenty of energy, enthusiasm and interesting ideas. They place great importance on accomplishment in life and they have a strong desire for the security of material success. They are multi-talented individuals with the determination to overcome any obstacle in pursuit of their goals and the only real barrier to their accomplishing anything they put their minds to is a tendency to scatter their energies too wide and lose focus.

The Xin You is a powerful character with equally powerful convictions, but they also have a very sensitive core. The powerful Friend Star 比肩星 in the form of the You 酉 (Rooster) is also a *Peach Blossom Star* 桃花星. This means they have the power to mesmerize and attract others. They may be quite vulnerable to criticism and they will need to develop faith in their own abilities if they are to reach their full potential.

With a love of family and a yearning for a firm foundation from which to springboard their ideas and explorations, the Xin You individual is likely to work to build a stable home. This is because the You 酉 (Rooster) inherently pulls-in the Chen 辰 (Dragon), a Direct Resource Star 正印星. They are capable of being very supportive and they may at times be a little controlling, though it is with good intentions for the betterment of his/her family.

The biggest life lesson for the Xin You may, in fact, be to learn to prioritise their relationships and to make the best use of their people skills. The Xin You individual is very sensitive and very intuitive. Helpful and friendly, they are also naturally insightful and understanding. They have a gift for tact and diplomacy and they can be an inspiration and a tower of strength to many. They are likely to gain a great deal of emotional satisfaction out of loaning their power and insight to others, however, they are likely to need to work to overcome a certain self-centredness and selfishness that their extreme self-reliance may give them. If they can use their instincts as a guide in finding a way to reconcile their need for self-expression with their wish for positive connections they are likely to discover a deeper sense of personal fulfilment.

Metal Rooster

Technical Observations

In this Chart, the Thriving 祿 of Xin 辛 is located at You 酉 (Rooster). If the Water element is present without the Mao 卯 (Rabbit), this will endow the individual with many great and honourable qualities. As long as Water is present in the Chart, Xin You can effectively use the Mao 卯 (Rabbit) Branch. This suggests an individual who has great affinity with money and the ability to establish his/her business empire.

The nature of Xin You will always clash with the Mao 卯 (Rabbit) and this will have a detrimental effect particularly for the male. Without the Water, a clash between the Mao 卯 (Rabbit) and the You 酉 (Rooster) indicates betrayal, hurt feelings and lack of focus in life. A Punishment 刑 formation is undesirable for this Chart, as this denotes potential breakups in partnerships; while a Clash 沖 by excessive Wood 木 denotes possible accidents.

It would be favourable if the Pillar meets with additional Metal 金 and Water 水 elements in the Luck Pillars. This is because it signifies smooth financial rewards for the individual of this Pillar.

The Xin You Day Pillar will benefit from the presence of a Ding 丁 Fire Stem. The Ding Fire helps sharpen and purify the Xin You Metal, making it shines brightly - akin to the jewellery glittering like stardust. This is indicative of fame and success in life. However, if the Xin is seen cutting through the Wood element without Ding Fire or any of the Water elements, it suggests that the individual may not be able to achieve any of his financial goals or he/she has very poor self-esteem.

Those individuals that are born in the Spring and Summer seasons, are likely to be blessed with a calm and peaceful life without too many challenges while longevity may be the blessing for those born during the Autumn and Winter seasons.

Those Xin You born during the day time (5AM - 5PM) may face some struggles in the early part of their life before finding success in their middle age. Those born in the night time (5PM - 5AM) are likely to be very fortunate and they have the potential to achieve wealth and success. It is inauspicious, however, for the Xin You to be born in the Xu 戌 (Dog) month. They are likely to find that they often have to battle with petty minded people who may work to undermine their success. They may also find that they encounter more obstacles and setbacks in life than their peers.

Unique 60 Pillar Combinations

This section covers the relationships between the individual pillar under this elemental polarity and several other pillars found in the 60 Jia Zi cycle.

Xin
You

Na Yin Death and Extinct 納音死絕
Xin You 辛酉 (Metal Rooster) + Bing Wu 丙午 (Fire Horse)

The Na Yin 納音 is also known as the Melodic Element of a Pillar. This Pillar will have a strong influence on the individual's subconscious mind. This Pillar will also affect the way people feel, perceive, or remember information and experiences.

An individual may encounter this Na Yin Death and Extinct Pillar if it appears in their BaZi Natal Chart in either the Year, Month, or Hour Pillars, the Luck Pillar, or the Annual Pillar.

If this configuration is found in the Year Pillar, the individual is likely to feel a lack of affinity with their grandparents. The relationship may be quite emotionally distant even if they live in close proximity. There is possibility that the relationship could even be completely estranged and that they no longer speak to their grandparents. The individual's friendships are affected as well, as the Year Pillar represents one's social circle. This could mean that there is a sense of detachment in their friendship with others and that the individual cannot rely or trust his/her friends.

If this configuration is present in the Month Pillar, the individual is likely to feel that they lack for an affinity with their parents. They may struggle to form a connection with their parents and they might find that their views and opinions are too disparate to reconcile. Again it's possible that they will be completely out of contact. The Month Pillar also governs career and a configuration here could also suggest that the individual lacks engagement with their career. Equally they may struggle to form positive working relationships with their colleagues.

When this configuration is found in the Hour Pillar, the individual may well lack for a feeling of affinity with their children. This could suggest that they are bringing up children who are not biologically their own due to marriage or adoption. Alternatively their children may be being brought up in another household. As the Hour Pillar also signifies one's hopes and dreams, this configuration also has a bearing on ideas and contributions and it is possible that the individual will be drifting through life without any real sense of purpose. They may have little idea about who they really are and what they stand for.

In the Luck Pillar, this configuration indicates a ten-year cycle in which the individual will lack for any kind of intuition or sixth sense. They may find that they suffer from depression and that they have feelings of anxiety and worry as they struggle to make sense of events. It is possible that they will believe they are always misinterpreting events and people and that nothing makes a great deal of sense. They are advised to ask for the support and guidance of trusted friends and family.

If this configuration is found in the Annual Pillar, it indicates an unsettled year of being haunted by unnamed worries and concerns. The individual will feel anxious and even hopeless but they will be unable to locate the source of these emotions.

Heaven Combine Earth Harm 天合地害
Xin You 辛酉 (Metal Rooster) + Bing Xu 丙戌 (Fire Dog)

In this configuration, the Bing Xu 丙戌 forms the Heaven Combine Earth Harm with the Day Pillar. The connection with the Heavenly Stem would seem to create a positive outlook, but the Harm formation carries negative emotions. The interpretation here is that whatever appearance of happiness the individual chooses to project, they will be hiding feelings uncertainty and distrust.

An individual may encounter this Heaven Combine Earth Harm Pillar if it appears in their Natal BaZi Chart in either the Year, Month, or Hour, the Luck Pillar, or the Annual Pillar.

If this configuration is found in the Year, Month or Hour Pillars, it indicates feelings of confusion and fear over the loyalty of various people in the individual's life. If this configuration is present in the Year Pillar, these feelings will be connected to their grandparents. It is possible that they do not have a strong bond with their grandparents or that they have never met them. As the Year Pillar also governs one's social circle, the individual may also face difficulty connecting with their friends or could feel alienated by them.

The Month Pillar represents one's work and career. If found in the Month Pillar, this configuration will indicate the relationship between the individual and their managers and supervisors at work, which may impede their career progression due to the lack of support and recognition. Their affinity with their parents is also affected and this configuration here would mean that they are not close despite appearances.

Metal
Rooster

If found in the Hour Pillar, these concerns the sense of loyalty related to their children, clients or staff. In each case, the individual will be confused about the relationship and they will be concerned that their trust may be misplaced. They may worry that these people would not be there for them in a crisis or they may be equally anxious that their confidences would be betrayed. Alternatively they may not feel free to be completely themselves with these people for fear of being rejected if they were completely honest. As the Hour Pillar is representative of one's ideas and dreams, it could mean that this individual has lost their direction in life and does not know what to do to move forward.

If this configuration is found in the Luck Pillar, it is an indication that an apparently positive and successful period will leave the individual feeling like a victim. They will be unable to find peace or pride in their achievements and they are likely to feel quite jaded and cynical about their careers and working relationships. They may believe that their accomplishments have come at a cost to them and that the price was too high to pay, no amount of financial compensation will ease their mind.

If this configuration is seen in the Annual Pillar, it suggests that a very promising year will end in disappointment. It is likely that the individual will become jealous when they compare their accomplishments with those of another and find them wanting. They are advised to look again and reassess, they have achieved enough, it is envy alone that is distorting their judgement and altering their perception.

Heaven Friend Earth Clash 天比地冲
Xin You 辛酉 (Metal Rooster) + Xin Mao 辛卯 (Metal Rabbit)

When the Xin Mao and Day Pillar meet they form the Heaven Friend Earth Clash Pillar. This indicates a situation in which an initial agreement will turn sour and escalate into dispute following changes in circumstance. Individuals with this Pillar in their Chart may find that their efforts fail to produce the progress they have been hoping for. They will be frequently very busy, with an active schedule but for all that they will not be achieving anything of note.

This Pillar is also an indication that promises fall short of expectation and cherished plans fail to follow the anticipated course. The individual may be wise to keep an open mind; the unexpected is not always bad. If the Heavenly Stem is favourable, even an apparently negative turn of events could have positive ramifications.

When this configuration appears in the Year, Month or Hour Pillars it is an indication that unexpected events or surprising pieces of news will have an impact on the individual's relationships. If this configuration is seen in the Year Pillar, there will be surprising twists and turns in the individual's relationships with their grandparents. It is possible that misunderstandings or conflict has tarnished their bond. Similar scenarios can be said to this individual's friendships as the Year Pillar also governs a person's social circle.

If seen in the Month Pillar, this configuration indicates that the individual may find their relationship with their parents unsettled by unforeseen circumstances. Equally they may find that their career path is altered by a change in perspective or an unexpected event, as the configuration in the Month Pillar also affects one's work and career.

Metal Rooster

In the Hour Pillar, the individual may find that they quarrel with their children following an unanticipated turn of events. Or it could be that their business and working relationships are placed in jeopardy by a change in the market. Alternatively there is a possibility that their eyes will be opened to new possibilities and they will change their ideas about life, as the Hour Pillar also governs one's hopes and dreams.

In each case the unexpected may well feel unsettling and unwelcome at the time but if the Heavenly Stem is favourable, the ultimate outcome will prove to be beneficial and these relationships may actually be enhanced.

If this configuration is present in the Luck Pillar, it is an indication of a period of steady change. The individual may face a difficult and painful time. There will be obstacles to face and they will find that their perspectives change. The decade will be one of growth and progression and the individual should be reassured that, however unlikely it may feel at the time, they will feel the benefits in the long term.

In the Annual Pillar, this configuration indicates a period of self-discovery. There will be surprises and unexpected events at every turning and the individual may have to wrestle with their emotions as they try to process new information and new perspectives. They will learn a great deal about themselves and be enriched by the experience.

Heaven and Earth Clash 天沖地沖
Xin You 辛酉 (Metal Rooster) + Ding Mao 丁卯 (Fire Rabbit)

This Heaven and Earth Clash Pillar is a configuration in which the Day Pillar is clashed by the Ding Mao 丁卯 Pillar. This is known as the Fan Yin 反吟 formation, and it is an unlucky formation as it will act to diminish any of the good qualities of an individual's Day Pillar. An individual with this Pillar in their chart may find that are constantly coming up against challenges that they are ill-equipped to face.

This configuration will have a negative effect on the Xin Mao even if it appears in someone else's chart. If this pillar appears in the chart of anyone connected to the Xin Mao, it is an indication that this person is likely to have a negative influence on their career. It could be that they will be a distraction, or they may be the source of poor, even if well-meaning, advice.

When seen in the Natal Chart, this configuration indicates a lack of affinity with the individuals or concepts represented by the specific Pillar in which it appears.

The Year Pillar represents grandparents and friends and a position here is likely to indicate that the individual will not have a particularly close relationship with their grandparents. The relationship may be rather cold and formal. Alternatively they might find it hard to make friends and they may feel quite lonely and misunderstood.

The Month Pillar represents authority figures and career. It's possible that the individual will be unable to connect with their parents, they may have very disparate views and this may lead to quarrels. Equally they might find that they cannot seem to earn the appreciation of their managers no matter how hard they work. It is possible that they will struggle even to find work.

Metal Rooster

The Hour Pillar represents dependants, employees and other working relationships, ideas and contributions. A position here could suggest that the individual finds that they are failing to understand their children. Alternatively they might not be able to develop a good rapport with their clients and this may impede their ability to meet their targets. They could even feel that they have completely lost step with the world.

Where this configuration is present in the Luck Pillar, the individual is likely to go through a very difficult and challenging time. They may feel that everything is going wrong and that they are facing almost insurmountable odds to achieve their goals. It would be advisable for them to find comfort and support in their trusted friendships.

In the Annual Pillar, this configuration suggests that the individual will face a period of time in which it would be very unwise for them to begin any new project or relationship. The indications are that they will have very poor luck during the year and they are recommended to keep a low profile. They should avoid making any major decisions or significant changes where possible.

Heaven Counter Earth Clash 天剋地冲
Xin You 辛酉 (Metal Rooster) + Yi Mao 乙卯 (Wood Rabbit)

This Heaven Counter Earth Clash Pillar is a configuration in which the Day Pillar is going against the Yi Mao 乙卯. It is important to note that this configuration and the Heaven and Earth Clash formations are different. In this situation the individual, rather than being diminished, is empowered and given a need for control. The Xin You individual with this configuration in their chart will have passion and a strong desire to win. They are likely to be dominant characters with an entrepreneurial spirit who have the potential to achieve great success but they must be careful not to be impatient or over hasty in their decision making.

An individual may encounter this Heaven Counter Earth Clash Pillar if it appears in their Natal Chart in either the Year, Month, or Hour Pillar, as well as the Luck Pillars, or the Annual Pillar.

When this configuration is seen in the Year Pillar, the individual may be helped to build upon their hard work with the assistance of high-profile friends. These people might be able to provide useful advice and invaluable information.

It this combination is found in the Month Pillar, the individual will almost certainly be money minded with a flair for business. They will have the drive and the ability to become very wealthy indeed but they may need to guard against become avaricious.

Metal Rooster

In the Hour Pillar, this configuration indicates that the individual will focus on their career to the exclusion of their personal relationships. They are advised to remember that lasting happiness and real fulfilment require more than career success and that they should not neglect their familial responsibilities.

When found in the Luck Pillar, this configuration suggests that the individual will be driven to pursue career success and they will have the skills to make their achievements substantial. They are likely to have an entrepreneurial spirit and a flair for investment and finances. There is a good chance that they will accumulate a great deal of material wealth but they are advised to think clearly before making a decision and to keep a level head.

When this configuration occurs in the Annual Pillar, it is very likely that the individual will encounter a myriad of opportunities for investment and career progression. They may begin a new venture or become involved in new partnerships or investments. They are likely to be able to reap the financial rewards but they should be warned that although the year may be very fruitful, it is also likely to be stressful and their personal relationships may suffer.

Heaven and Earth Unity 天同地比
Xin You 辛酉 (Metal Rooster) + Xin You 辛酉 (Metal Rooster)

If you see another Xin You in the Chart it will form the Fu Yin 伏吟 configuration, otherwise known as the Heaven and Earth Unity, which is a sad indication of sorrow and emotional events. It is often referred to as the hidden warning Pillar.

An individual may encounter this Fu Yin formation if it appears in their BaZi Natal Chart in either the Year Pillar, the Month Pillar, or the Hour Pillar, the Luck Pillar or the Annual Pillar.

When this configuration is present in the Year Pillar, the individual is likely to have a very distant relationship with their grandparents. Even if they live near to them they will be unable to develop much of a connection, it is also possible that they may never have met their grandparents. The individual may also have a detached relationship with his/her friends, if the configuration appears in the Year Pillar, which also governs one's social circle.

If found in the Month Pillar, this configuration suggests that the individual will have a very poor relationship with their parents. There may be bitterness connected to an inability to inherit or take over a family business. It's possible that the relationship will have been completely estranged. As the Month Pillar also governs one's work and career, the configuration here would mean that the individual may not receive much support or recognition from his/her superiors and peers. This will therefore impedes the individual's career progression.

If this configuration appears in the Hour Pillar, a disconnection with children is indicated. It is possible that the individual will have no desire to have children or they may desire it profoundly and be unable. Alternatively they may have been separated from their children, who are being brought up by their grandparents or a previous partner. The Hour Pillar also represents one's hopes and dreams, and this could indicate that the individual has no sense of purpose or direction in life, or does not have the means or ability to realize their goals.

In the Luck Pillar, this configuration signifies a spiritual path and indeed this is often called the spiritual Pillar. The individual may become devoutly religious and they may even choose to follow a religious calling. It is sadly also possible that they will lose a parent. The final alternative is that they might become very preoccupied with their health and they will devote their time to diet and exercise.

If this configuration is found in the Annual Pillar, the individual is likely to achieve a great deal during the year. They will see progress in their careers and they will almost certainly see a corresponding increase in their material wealth. They may also choose to invest in property. There is also however a prediction that at least one emotionally straining event will overshadow the year.

Heaven and Earth Combine 天地相合
Xin You 辛酉 (Metal Rooster) + Bing Chen 丙辰 (Fire Dragon)

The Heaven and Earth Combine is the most desirable of all of the Pillars to be seen in a BaZi Chart. This configuration brings connectivity and positive relationships. Individuals with this Pillar in their Chart are very likely to be happy and successful.

If this configuration is found in the charts of people connected to the Xin You it is an indication that these people will have a positive influence and they will be able to offer help and support

An individual may encounter this Heaven and Earth Combine Pillar if it appears in their BaZi Natal Chart in either the Year, Month, or Hour Pillars, the Luck Pillar, or the Annual Pillar.

If this configuration is present in the Year Pillar, the individual is likely to find peace and comfort in the company of their grandparents. They will also benefit from good and loyal friends and an active social life. Their popularity will mean that they have a good social standing and they will be able to open doors and make the right contacts.

When seen in the Month Pillar, this configuration is an indication that the individual will enjoy the confidence and security that only a firm foundation can provide. They will appreciate the love and support of their parents. They are also likely to be passionate about their careers and they will have the respect and admiration of their colleagues

If this configuration is found in the Hour Pillar, the individual will have a wonderful relationship with their children. Their happy home will provide a positive foundation for the next generation. These individuals are also likely to be able to build a secure working environment through their positive relationships with their employees, customers and suppliers.

In either the Luck Pillar or the Annual Pillar, this configuration suggests that the individual will experience positive relationships in all areas of their life bringing them material and emotional wealth. They will be lucky in love, find harmony in marriage and be professionally successful through partnerships and joint ventures.

Metal Rooster

Heaven Friend Earth Punish 天比地刑
Xin You 辛酉 (Metal Rooster) + Xin You 辛酉 (Metal Rooster)

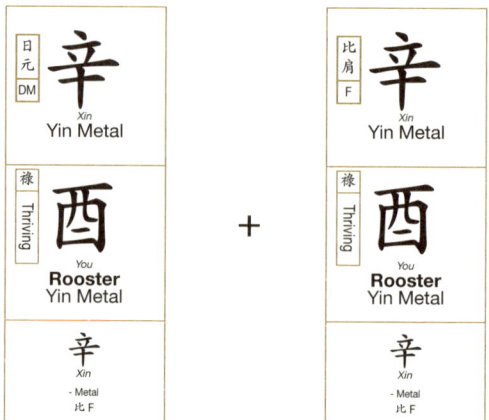

The Heaven Friend Earth Punish Pillar is very similar to the Heaven Combine Earth Punish Pillar. The difference here is that the Heavenly Stem does not form a Combination. The Friend Star 比肩星 appears in the Stem and this indicates that the self is the key theme of this Pillar.

This is the Pillar of personal discovery and experience. The Earthly Branch forms a Punishment which suggests that the individual is likely to experience feelings of tension and stress. A Punishment formation also often means that there will be emotional pain to be endured, however, in this situation it is likely to be self-inflicted.

An individual may encounter this Heaven Friend Earth Punish Pillar if it appears in their Natal BaZi Chart in either the Year, Month, or Hour Pillars, the Luck Pillar, or the Annual Pillar.

If this configuration is found in the Year Pillar, the individual will probably feel very insecure about their relationship with their grandparents. However warm or pleasant the relationship might be, they will still feel that they are unable to give enough. It is possible that they will worry that their grandparents aren't proud of them or they may be anxious that they will not be able to provide their grandparents with enough time and care as they age. The Year Pillar also represents a person's social circle and this could mean that they find it difficult to form a close bond with people or that they question their friendship with others due to their own insecurity.

If this configuration is present in the Month Pillar, the individual will experience the same insecurity in connection to their relationship with their parents. The individual is very likely to fear that they will not be able to fulfil their parents' hopes and expectations; they will think this way regardless of what their parents actually feel. As the Month Pillar also governs one's career and work life, it can indicate an individual who is constantly affected by work related stress. They are may struggle to be able to connect with their colleagues and they will feel overwhelmed by their workload. They will not believe that they are adequate to the task.

In the Hour Pillar, this configuration suggests that the individual will be quite anxious about their parenting skills. They will worry that they are not providing enough material or emotional support or that they are not giving enough time. Everyone else will be able to see that they have a good relationship with their children and that they are happy and healthy but the Xin You will not believe it. The Hour Pillar also represents a person's hopes and ideas, and this could reflect the individual who lacks faith in their abilities to achieve their goals.

Metal Rooster

If this configuration is found in the Luck Pillar, the individual is likely to be very successful but their pride and confidence will be wounded when they face challenges that are far greater than they had anticipated. This will form part of a decade of learning in which the individual will face some trying times and their patience and trust will be tested. They are advised to remain focused and not allow themselves to be distracted or demoralised.

In the Annual Pillar, this configuration indicates a year in which the individual will be attracted to a series of playful and flirtatious new relationships. They are unlikely to find the love of their life but they may find that they are distracted from their goals. Though the year has the potential to offer opportunities for fun and pleasure, the individual may be wise to work their priorities and maintain focused on their long term aspirations.

Mutual Exchange Goat Blade 互換羊刃
Xin You 辛酉 (Metal Rooster) + Geng Xu 庚戌 (Metal Dog)

When the Xin You meets with a Geng Xu 庚戌 it is called the Mutual Exchange Goat Blade Pillar, and this has the similar effect to meeting a Rob Wealth Goat Blade 劫財羊刃. Instead of effecting wealth, however, this configuration will have an impact on the individuals' physical wellbeing. They may find that their health will deteriorate and they may be involved in accidents. The chances of their being involved in an accident are likely to be increased if they are in the company of someone else who has this configuration in their Chart.

Rob Wealth Goat Blade 劫財羊刃
Xin You 辛酉 (Metal Rooster) + Geng Xu 庚戌 (Metal Dog)

If you are a Xin You, you do not want to see a Geng Xu 庚戌 Pillar in your Chart. This will form a Rob Wealth Goat Blade 劫財羊刃 formation, which is an indication of serious financial losses and emotional or relationship problems. People with this configuration in their chart may work very hard but find that their goals are unattainable. They will often be left feeing disappointed, exhausted and disillusioned.

Anyone will this configuration in their chart may be a cause of the Xin You losing money. This is unlikely to be because they are thieves and swindlers; it is quite possible that neither they nor the Xin You will be aware of what is happening at the time. The Xin You may even be happy to see the money go and not realize the impact until much later. It could be that these individuals may simply be entertaining companions and the Xin You is compelled to overspend when they are together. The Xin You may even enjoy spending money on them.

辛亥
Xin Hai

| 辛丑 | 辛卯 | 辛巳 | 辛未 | 辛酉 | 辛亥 |
| Xin Chou | Xin Mao | Xin Si | Xin Wei | Xin You | Xin Hai |

Getting to Know
Xin Hai 辛亥 (Metal Pig)

Positive Imagery

Negative Imagery

Getting to Know
Xin Hai 辛亥 (Metal Pig)

General Observations:

The imagery of jewellery naturally formed underwater like a pearl in an oyster represents the Xin Hai. The representation indicates beauty and one who is at peace and unshaken by any disruption.

Individuals under the Xin Hai 辛亥 tend to be highly creative and artistic. They are usually very attractive both physically and intellectually and can charm others easily. Innately talented, they are highly ambitious and usually feel that nothing is impossible.

When others first meet the Xin Hai, they immediately notice their fierce or straightforward, no-nonsense personality. However, when they get to know the Xin Hai better, they will find that Xin Hais are innately caring and respectful of others. Due to their determination and resilience, they make excellent leaders who are able to assess a situation quickly and think of the best course of action. They are excellent thinkers and strategists.

Other traits that help them to rise in the ranks of leadership include their tenacity and values. Their tenacious attitude motivates them to see all their tasks to completion, while their values ensure that any task they take on gets done right. They also ensure that they are well understood. This explains their straight forward and direct nature. However, at times this straight-forward nature of Xin Hais often gives the impression that they are impersonable or harsh.

When it comes to dealing with others, they are nurturing and warm hearted. Others are immediately charmed by their sociable and amiable nature. This works out well for the Xin Hai too because they crave affection and attention from their close friends and acquaintances.

Although they enjoy being social, they do require time alone to recharge their spirit. They are constantly working on themselves, which is why they spend much time in reflection, contemplation and meditation. Deep within, they are noble and have an altruistic approach to life. This life approach may lead them into spirituality and metaphysics.

Money can be an issue for the Xin Hai. Finances for them can easily fluctuate. In their early years, the Xin Hai may have trouble saving money or accumulating wealth. There are many reasons for this, one of the main reasons being their extravagant streak. As they become older, their finances should improve. By the time they reach their later stages of life, they will be able to savour prosperity. It is a good idea for them to create a smart savings or financial plan for when the unexpected happens.

Under pressure, the Xin Hai tend to be impatient, worried, and indecisive. These three personal obstacles can stand in the way of their achievements. These negative traits can also cause the Xin Hai to waste their energy pursuing unworthy goals. This wasted energy may cause them to experience restlessness and self-doubt. Channelling their energy and becoming more disciplined will help them to turn their dreams into reality.

It is important that the Xin Hai not allow themselves to make hasty decisions by taking on something that they later regret. Eventually, they may drop the project all together.

Xin Hais are innately driven by emotions. On the surface they may seem to act on logic but in truth, they are influenced by their deep emotions. They can be practically unshakable once they've made up their minds about something.

The Xin Hai are prone to boredom if they do not receive constant mental and emotional stimulation to keep them on their toes. Otherwise, they can easily lose focus and interest on their initial endeavours or intentions and move on to new things that capture their attention.

Key Character Traits of the Xin Hai 辛亥: Overall

- Intelligent
- Witty
- Self-Doubting
- Loving
- Caring
- Honest
- Sensitive
- Precise
- Attractive

Work Life

Xin
Hai

Professional Self

These individuals will easily find success in many different professions due to their multiple talents and skills. They are perfectionists and will always do their jobs to the best of their ability. This trait is invaluable to their career development and allows them to work great in positions of leadership and management.

Their keen intellect allows them to pick up on new ideas easily. Innovating and spearheading new industries is where they will find the most success.

With an authoritative nature, they will be highly successful in the business world. Others immediately notice their commanding presence and as a result, are confident and eager to follow them.

Despite their diligence, they must avoid any work where there is monotony. In order to remain satisfied, their position must provide flexibility.

Because they are very particular and precise, they must have an organized working environment. Signs of disorder and inadequacy will likely cause them great frustration.

Career Options

Xin Hai individuals are multi-talented. Professions that will utilize their eye for precision such as science or engineering are ideal. With their innate business sense, Xin Hai individuals would also have exceptional careers in banking, real estate or fund management.

Their good communication skills suggest that they would be successful dealing in the public sector. This would include careers in politics, law, counselling, psychology, or social work.

If they need to satisfy their yearning for creative and artistic expression, the Xin Hai could make a successful career in any artistic related endeavour. Their artistic eye and masterful storytelling skills would make them great in careers involving acting, music, film, media or any form of entertainment.

With a genuine joy for learning and sharing knowledge, the Xin Hai would make excellent teachers, or lecturers. They could also use this same joy to become a consultant or advisor.

Metal Pig

Metal Pig

Key Character Traits of the Xin Hai 辛亥: Work life

Positive

- Responsible
- Intuitive
- Creative
- Optimistic
- Independent
- Gregarious
- Compassionate

Negative

- Insecure
- Withdrawn
- Reclusive
- Eccentric
- Over Sensitive
- Jealous
- Impatient

Love and Relationships

Xin
Hai

Love

Xin Hai individuals are generally good-looking and have no trouble attracting many interested suitors.

They hold high expectations for their relationships. Because of this, they may choose to experiment with different kinds of partners. Ultimately, they are in search of partners who they can share an exciting bond with.

Ideally, the Xin Hai needs a partner who is compassionate, abiding, patient, intelligent and understanding. They prefer a partner who can satisfy them mentally and intellectually. They also want someone who will be able to understand and take care of their gentle and emotional nature. Once they are in love, they are idealistic and willing to make sacrifices.

Generally, they are nervous and restless when it comes to romantic relationships. They are often indecisive which can lead to a lot of polarizing behaviour in the relationship. One moment, they may appear enthusiastic and passionate and the next moment, they may appear cold and uninterested.

They must be cautious not to appear too detached. Detachment is usually an exterior mask of deeper emotions of jealously and suspiciousness.

Acquaintances

Xin Hai individuals are sociable, friendly and entertaining. As great communicators, they truly enjoy mixing and mingling with many different types of people.

Being a part of a group is highly important to their mental stimulation. Nothing pleases the Xin Hai more than being able to learn new things from others.

As they tend to be very wise, others seek them for advice. Because of their sensitive, yet honest nature, they will gladly share their thoughts and opinions with them.

They have an impeccable way with people. However, they must be careful of their tendency to be bossy and critical. This will make others feel inferior and ultimately damage their closest and most valuable relationships.

Metal Pig

Family

When it comes to marriage it is better for Xin Hai individuals to wait. Later marriages give the Xin Hai time enough to mature. Also, later marriages are likely to have a more favourable outcome as the Xin Hai knows how to better control their emotions.

Once they do find their life partner, they are devoted, and loyal. They make every effort to include their partner in their decisions and will hold their opinions to high regards.

Marriage for the female Xin Hai is less probable than their male counterpart, and she is more likely to remain single. Her outspokenness and abrupt nature may turn off many potential suitors. Such behaviour may stem from her inner insecurities and she needs to overcome it if she desire to settle down one day. Compared to most people, she may take a longer time to find an ideal partner, but the chances are higher if she travels more.

While the Xin Hai individuals do strive for peace, they can become jealous and short tempered. They must not allow insecurity and self-doubt to ruin an otherwise successful marriage.

Key Character Traits of the Xin Hai 辛亥: Love & Relationships

- Marriage is better later in life
- Many different social groups are likely
- Desire protection in relationships
- Attracted to compassionate and protective people
- Nervous and restless

Famous Personalities

Hussein Onn - The 3rd Prime Minister of Malaysia, and is known as the Father of Unity. He comes from a family of deep nationalistic and political roots. He was also a lawyer.

Charles Ergen - American businessman and co-founder of the satellite dish provider, Dish Network.

Source: Wikipedia (June 2013)

Metal Pig

Technical Analysis

Xin
Hai

BaZi Day Pillar Analytics 日柱分析

時 Hour	日 Day	月 Month。	年 Year	
	辛 Xin Yin Metal (日元 DM)			天干 Heavenly Stems
	亥 Hai Pig Yin Water (沐 Bath)			地支 Earthly Branches
	壬 Ren +Water 傷 HO ／ 甲 Jia +Wood 財 DW			藏干 Hidden Stems

辛亥 Metal Pig

Description

Xin 辛 Metal and Hai 亥 (Pig/Water) is in a harmoniously balanced configuration. This suggests that the individual will boast academic and literary credentials, though this is more likely to be true for the male than for the female. The Bath 沐浴 position (of the *12 Growth and Birth Phases of BaZi*) of the Xin 辛 Stem is located at Hai 亥. The Hai 亥 Branch in turn contains the prosperous Hurting Officer Star 傷官星, which also suggests that the Xin Hai will have a rather strong, dominating and forceful character. For the male Xin Hai, this is often a good indication as it is favourable for him to attain success in his career undertakings. And in some ways, this setting also means that they are likely to marry a beautiful and successful woman since the Branch of the Pillar represents the Spouse Palace. For the female Xin Hai however, it may be a less favourable sign in terms of marriage as she may have difficulty in finding a man to match her strong personality.

Metal Pig

The Xin Hai are exciting individuals. They have strong emotions and opinions. They are adventurous with a love of travel and meeting new people. This is the effect of the Hai 亥 (Pig) which is a *Travelling Star*, a star of mobility. They are highly independent but also very gregarious. They enjoy having new experiences and tend to have very active social calendars.

Xin Hai individuals have exceptionally sharp and fast minds. They learn very quickly and enjoy putting their knowledge to practical applications. They have strong reasoning powers and are able to think creatively to develop innovative solutions. All this thanks to the power of the Hurting Officer Star 傷官星 and the Direct Wealth Star 正財星 in the Hai (Pig) Branch. As these two Stars are in the elements of Water and Wood, in a harmonious *producing-relationship*, Xin Hais are extraordinarily witty and intelligent. Courageous and pioneering, they are likely to strike out on their own accord to make a 'little dent' in the universe.

The Xin Hai has a capacity to self-start and a sensitivity that, when combined, often loan them keen leadership abilities. They are intuitive and understanding with excellent people skills. All this thanks to the Water natured Hurting Officer Star. They are often very receptive with a natural appreciation of the needs and motivations of others. They may be able to use tact and diplomacy to encourage those around them in cooperative endeavours. They are also often able to inspire others to find their way and be the best that they can be.

Xin Hai individuals have a deep need for people that can sometimes work to their detriment. This is because the Xin Metal inherent *silent-pulls* a Bing 丙 Fire, while the Hai 亥 (Pig) Branch *silent-clashes* a Si 巳 (Snake) which is also the Bing 丙 Fire. This pull-push relationship of the Bing Fire suggests that the Xin Hai inherently yearns for attention and affection, and when they do get it, they subconsciously push it away.

Metal Pig

They may sometimes forget to find a balance between their work and their busy social lives. In addition, though they have a keen sense of independence and a desire to establish their own unique identity, they may find that they allow themselves to be overly influenced by their peer groups. This is caused by the fact that Hai 亥 (Pig) silent clashes away the Si 巳 (Snake) - which is the *Growth Branch of Metal* 金之長生 - representing Friends to the Xin Metal. They often allow the negativity of others to hold them back and they may sometimes need to work on developing confidence in their own convictions.

Intelligent and well-educated with a wide range of interests the Xin Hai can sometimes be guilty of spreading themselves too thin. They see so much to be inspired by that they can sometimes lack for focus. They can also be inclined toward allowing their emotions to cloud their judgement and this may prevent them from being able to make the most of their skills. It will be important for them to obtain a sense of calm and discipline in order to find success and fulfilment.

Technical Observations

For the Xin Hai 辛亥, the combination of Yin 寅 (Tiger) and Hai 亥 (Pig) in their BaZi Chart is known as *Filtering Gold with a Sieve Formation* (撈金用篩) or *Landing on the Opposite Shore Formation*(登彼岸). What this means is that the gold, with all its shinning glory, is essentially useless if it is buried under the mud. This is also because the Tiger and Pig Branches form a Punishment Storage 刑庫 formation in the Chart.

Women born under the Xin Hai Day Pillar may have difficulty in finding a husband. Even if they do find one, it doesn't take them long to drive him away. This is because of the presence of the Hai 亥 (Pig) in their Chart, which reflects away the Sun. (In the study of BaZi, Hai 亥 (Pig) clashes the Si 巳(Snake), which contains Bing Fire. The Sun, in this case is represented by Bing 丙 Fire. Bing Fire is the Direct Officer Star 正官星, which symbolises the husband in the Chart. As the sun enters, its light is reflected away (Hai contains Ren 壬 Water Hurting Officer Star 傷官星, which is like a river reflecting the sunlight, and as such it serves to drive any potential suitors away.) Xin Hai women must be wary to not bring forth the full power of their Hurting Officer 傷官 Star in their Chart. These women may need to learn to control the aggressive nature of their temperament and become more understanding and patient. The Xin Hai has a very powerful Hurting Officer Star 傷官星, as Ren 壬 Water covers 75% of the planet. For good marriage luck to happen for this Xin Metal lady, the Hai 亥 (Pig) in the Chart has to be removed first.

It is favourable for this Pillar if it meets with the Yin 寅, Wu 午, Xu 戌 and Fire 火 elements in the Luck Pillars. However, conversely, the Shen 申, Zi 子, Chen 辰 and Water 水 elements in the Luck Pillars should be avoided for as it may have a negative effect on their relationships. In order for an individual with this Day Pillar to become wealthy, they will require a favorable combination of the Mao 卯 (Rabbit) and Hai 亥 (Pig).

The configuration of Bing 丙 with the Xin 辛 Stem is more favourable for women as it tends to mean that they are very beautiful. If a woman is beautiful enough to attract the Sun (Bing Fire), Wood (the Wealth Star) will grow and this is an indication of prosperity and happiness in marriage. In this scenario any husband will be deeply devoted to their wife and they will have a sincere and conservative relationship. The effect on the male Xin Hai is less favourable as it will act to curb their power and make them more reserved.

辛亥 Metal Pig

Unique 60 Pillar Combinations

This section covers the relationships between the individual pillar under this elemental polarity and several other pillars found in the 60 Jia Zi cycle.

Xin
Hai

Heaven Combine Earth Harm 天合地害
Xin Hai 辛亥 (Metal Pig) + Bing Shen 丙申 (Fire Monkey)

The Heaven Combine Earth Harm Pillar combines with the Heavenly Stem, but forms a Harm 害 with the Earthly Branch. The Heavenly Stem appears to indicate that the individual will be contented and prosperous but the Harm formation carries more sinister implications. In this case the individual is likely to be quite uncertain about their relationships. They may even be concerned that they are at risk of betrayal.

When this configuration is found in the Natal Chart, these negative emotions will be connected to the individuals or concepts that are represented by the specific Pillar in which it appears.

The Year Pillar represents grandparents and friends. A position here would suggest that the individual does not feel entirely secure in one or both of these relationships. It could be that they are not able to be completely open with their grandparents and fear a rejection if they told them the truth. Alternatively it could be that their friends are prone to gossip and so the Xin Hai is unable to confide them.

The Month Pillar represents authority figures and career. A position here could suggest that the individual feels that they cannot trust their parents. It may be a similar situation to the above in which the individual fears that their parents would turn their back on them if they failed to live up to expectation. Equally the individual may feel that their colleagues at work may take credit for their ideas or their managers would fail to support them in a crisis.

The Hour Pillar represents children and employees, customers and clients as well as ideas and contributions. A position here may indicate that the individual fears that their children are not being honest with them. Alternatively their employees may be misusing company time or they might have reason to be concerned about the loyalty of their customers. They could equally become disillusioned with their direction in life.

If this configuration is found in the Luck Pillar, success and achievement will result in feelings of victimisation rather than pride. The individual is likely to feel rather cynical about their work and colleagues. It is likely that they will feel that their accomplishments came at a cost to them and no amount of financial compensation will bring them peace.

In the Annual Pillar, this configuration is likely to indicate that a successful year will end in disappointment. The individual needs to think carefully about the source of their emotions, they are likely to have achieved enough and it is jealousy alone that is distorting their judgement and causing them to them deem their accomplishments insufficient. They need to learn not to compare themselves with others.

Heaven Friend Earth Clash 天比地冲
Xin Hai 辛亥 (Metal Pig) + Xin Si 辛巳 (Metal Snake)

The Heaven Friend Earth Clash Pillar indicates than an agreement will break down after a change in circumstances. Individuals with this Pillar in their Chart may appear to be very busy but all their activity is unlikely to result in any material progress. They are making empty efforts which are leading nowhere. This configuration suggests that promises will fail to be delivered and events will not unfold as anticipated, causing the individual to feel unsettled and dissatisfied. However it may be wise for the Xin Hai to keep an open mind, the unexpected may yet prove to be a positive if the Heavenly Stem is favourable.

Wherever this configuration appears, it brings with it the idea that unexpected turns of event will lead to disagreements and disappointments in connection again to the represented individuals and concepts.

In the Year Pillar, this configuration will suggest that a change in circumstances will act to unsettle the individual's relationship with their grandparents or with their friends. It could be that a conflict or misunderstanding had suddenly surfaced with either the grandparents or in their social circle, which may possibly sever their connection if no genuine efforts were made to resolve matters.

In the Month Pillar, it will instead be their relationship with their parents. Some unexpected news or a change in situation may throw the relationship into chaos. As the Month Pillar also represents a person's work and career, this configuration here would mean that this individual and their supervisors at work may find themselves in constant disagreement. This would eventually impede the individual's career progression.

Finally a position in the Hour Pillar is an indication that the individual's relationship with their children or with their employees may change. Alternatively their understanding of their contribution to society may take a blow, as the Hour Pillar also represents one's ideas and hopes.

It is worth noting that in each of these cases the unsettling effects of these events and revelations may prove to be short lived if the Heavenly Stem is favourable, and they may yet prove to have the effect to improving and enhancing relationships.

If this configuration is seen in the Luck Pillar, the individual is likely to be faced with a learning period which will cause them to gradually change as a person. It will be a difficult, possibly even a painful time, but it will result in growth and progress and the ultimate outcome will prove to be a positive. The individual is advised to be patient and to have faith in their loved ones.

In the Annual Pillar, this configuration is likely to mean that the individual will live through a year of surprising twists and turns. It will be a very unsettling time and it may force the individual to reassess many of their fondly held beliefs. They will have to fight some private battles but ultimately they will be rewarded with self-knowledge and valuable experience.

Metal Pig

Heaven Friend Earth Punish 天比地刑
Xin Hai 辛亥 (Metal Pig) + Xin Hai 辛亥 (Metal Pig)

This Pillar is similar to the Heaven Combine and Earth Punish. However in this situation the Heavenly Stem doesn't form a configuration. A Friend Star 比肩星 instead appears in the Stem and this indicates that the self is the key theme of this Pillar.

This Pillar is one of personal experience. There is an indication of emotional pain, tension, and stress, but in keeping with the theme these are likely to be self-inflicted.

An individual may encounter this Heaven Friend Earth Punish if it appears in their BaZi Natal Chart in either the Year Pillar, the Month Pillar, or the Hour Pillar, the Luck Pillars or the Annual Pillar.

If this configuration is found in the Year Pillar, the individual is likely to have a warm and pleasant relationship with their grandparents, but they will nevertheless be afraid that they are not doing enough and that they are failing somehow. They may be concerned that they aren't able spare enough time to support their grandparents as they age.

A position in the Month Pillar suggests that whatever their parents may feel, the individual will still be insecure about the relationship and they will worry that they are unable to live up to their parents expectations. The Month Pillar also has a connection with the individual's career. A position here suggests that the individual will be experiencing a lot of work related stress. They will be tortured by the fear that they underperforming and will feel utterly inadequate to the task.

Metal Pig

Found in the Hour Pillar, this configuration suggests that the individual will have nagging doubts about their ability to provide for their children. They may appear to have a happy home and their children may be bight and contented by the individual will nevertheless be concerned their parenting abilities are lacking.

If this configuration is visible in the Luck Pillar, it indicates that unexpected challenges and setbacks are likely to cause the individual's confidence to suffer. This will all form part of a learning process in which the individual will find their patience and their faith tested. The individual is advised to keep calm and stay focused.

In the Annual Pillar, this configuration suggests that the individual will be drawn to a series of flirtations and infatuations. On the surface the year has the potential to be fun and light-hearted but the individual may need to be wary of being too distracted from their career goals, particularly if they are still working to establish a name and a reputation in their field.

Heaven and Earth Clash 天冲地冲
Xin Hai 辛亥 (Metal Pig) + Ding Si 丁巳 (Fire Snake)

This Heaven and Earth Clash Pillar is a configuration in which the Day Pillar is clashed by the Ding Si 丁巳 Pillar. This is known as the Fan Yin 反吟 formation and it is an unlucky formation because it will diminish any of the good qualities of an individual's Day Pillar. In addition to impairing the individual's chances of achieving their goals based on their own merits, this configuration may also act to place more obstacles in their path which they may not always be equipped to overcome.

Anyone connected to the Xin Hai with this configuration in their chart may well be found to be the source of poor advice. Though they may be kind and well-meaning they are likely to prove to be a bad influence and they are likely to have a detrimental effect on the individual's career.

Seen in the Natal Chart, this configuration indicates a lack of affinity with the individual or individuals represented by the specific Pillar in which it appears.

When seen in the Year Pillar, this configuration indicates that the individual will feel a lack of affinity with their grandparents. It may be that their grandparents do not understand the pressures of modern living or that the individual considers their grandparents' opinions old-fashioned and irrelevant. Alternatively the individual may struggle to form lasting friendships.

In the Month Pillar, this configuration suggests that the individual will lack for an affinity with their parents. An inability to communicate effectively may mean that the individual is unable to connect with their parents intellectually or emotionally. Alternatively the individual may be uninspired by their career path or they may not be able to form a positive working relationship with their supervisors and colleagues.

Should this configuration be present in the Hour Pillar, the individual may struggle to understand their children or it may be their employees that are mystery to them. Alternatively they may feel that they have lost step with the world and they do not know how to give something back to society.

When seen in the Luck Pillar, the effects of this configuration are most unfortunate. The individual is likely to live through quite a stressful decade. They will face challenges and setbacks at every turn and they may feel that nothing they touch turns out right. They are advised to take comfort in their friends.

If this configuration occurs in the Annual Pillar, it is recommended that the individual keep a low profile for the year. They should avoid making any major financial investments where possible and they should aim to maintain continuity in their personal and professional lives. It is likely that any new venture or relationship undertaken at this time will end badly. The individual is advised to be patient and wait for the time to pass.

Metal Pig

Heaven Counter Earth Clash 天剋地沖
Xin Hai 辛亥 (Metal Pig) + Yi Si 乙巳 (Wood Snake)

This Heaven Counter Earth Clash Pillar is a configuration in which the Day Pillar is going against the Yi Si 乙巳. It is important to note that this configuration and the Heaven and Earth Clash formations are different. In this situation, far from being diminished, the individual is empowered. They will have passion and a strong desire to be in control and to win. They are likely to be dominant characters with an entrepreneurial spirit who have the potential to achieve great success but they must be careful not to be impatient or over hasty in their decision making.

An individual may encounter this Heaven Counter Earth Clash Pillar if it appears in their Natal Chart in either the Year, Month, or Hour Pillar, as well as the Luck Pillars, or the Annual Pillar.

When the configuration is seen in the Year Pillar, the individual is likely to benefit from the assistance of high-profile friends in the form of useful advice and good guidance. Though this will not be a substitute for hard work, the insight that these people will be able to offer may prove invaluable.

If this configuration is found in the Month Pillar, the individual will almost certainly be business minded and will have a love of making money. They are driven by the adrenalin of success. These individual may be wise to guard against allowing avarice to become too great a motivation for them.

In the Hour Pillar, this configuration suggests that the individual will be a workaholic. These people may be wise to remember that healthy relationships form a part of a happy and balanced life and that they should not neglect their friendships or their familial responsibilities.

When found in the Luck Pillar, the configuration denotes an individual with the drive to succeed and the skill and acumen to acquire career success and material wealth. These individuals are likely to have an entrepreneurial flair and an eye for spotting a good investment. These individuals are advised to make the most of their good fortune while aiming to think carefully and keep a level head. Any risks taken should be calculated risks.

When this configuration occurs in the Annual Pillar, the individual is likely to encounter a myriad of opportunities to for investment and career progression. They may begin a new venture or become involved in new partnerships or investments. They should however be aware that, as much as, the year will be fruitful, it will also be stressful. While it would be prudent to work hard and take advantage of their success, the individual should also spare some time for their own well-being and that of their family.

Heaven and Earth Unity 天同地比
Xin Hai 辛亥 (Metal Pig) + Xin Hai 辛亥 (Metal Pig)

If you see another Xin Hai in the Chart, this forms a Fu Yin 伏吟 formation. This Heaven and Earth Unity formation is often an indication of sad emotional events, for this reason it is often referred to as the hidden warning Pillar.

An individual may encounter this Fu Yin formation if it appears in their BaZi Natal Chart in either the Year Pillar, the Month Pillar, or the Hour Pillar, the Luck Pillar or the Annual Pillar.

In the Year Pillar, this configuration indicates that, there will be a feeling of distance in the individual's relationship with their grandparents. The relationship may be rather strained and formal. It is equally possible that they may never have even met their grandparents.

If this configuration is found in the Month Pillar, it suggests that the individual will have a similarly strained and distant relationship with their parents. They may frequently quarrel or they may not speak at all. This may result from or lead to a situation with regard to inheritance or a family business. The individual's parents may be unwilling or unable to include them in their will, alternatively the individual may choose not to take on the family business and create a feeling of bitterness.

Metal Pig

When this configuration is found in the Hour Pillar, a level of distance with regard to children is symbolised. This may be a physical distance in that the children are being raised in another household by their grandparents or by a previous partner. Equally this may be an indication that the individual does not have children or that they find they are unable.

In the Luck Pillar, a spiritual path may be indicated by the presence of this Configuration. The individual may choose to take up a religious vocation or they may simply be very devout. Alternative spirituality could also be indicated or a focus of health related matters. The last, distressing, implication is that they may lose a parent.

If this configuration is found in the Annual Pillar, it suggests that the year will see career success and an increase in wealth and property. Sadly, however, these achievements may prove to be of little comfort in the face of loss and emotionally straining events.

Heaven and Earth Combine 天地相合
Xin Hai 辛亥 (Metal Pig) + Bing Yin 丙寅 (Fire Tiger)

When the Xin Hai and Bing Yin forms a Heaven and Earth Combine it carries with it very positive implications for the lucky Xin Hai in whose Chart it is seen. This is the most desirable configuration to find in a BaZi Chart. It is an indication that the individual will enjoy good connections in all areas of their life that will help to make them happy and successful.

Anyone connected to the Xin Hai individual with this Pillar is their Chart will enjoy a special affinity with them. They will be a good friend and a positive influence.

When this configuration is found in the Year Pillar the individual will have a warm relationship with their grandparents. They will appreciate the comfort and wise council that their grandparents are able to offer. They are also likely to be popular with a wide social circle and a good social standing which will help them to network. In amongst all their admirers, they will also benefit from close and loyal friends.

If this configuration occurs in the Month Pillar, the individual is likely to have an excellent relationship with their parents. They will never doubt that they will have the support of a stable family unit and their parents will always be proud of them. They are also likely to be passionate about their careers and respected in their fields. Their opinion will be heard and their efforts noticed.

In the Hour Pillar, this configuration is an indication of good parenting abilities. They will have a open and loving relationship with their children. They are also likely to be able to progress in their careers as they will have a unique ability to relate to their customers and clients and understand their specific needs and motivations.

If this configuration is seen in the Luck Pillar or the Annual Pillar, the individual is likely to enjoy relationship success in all areas of their life. They will achieve their career goals through partnerships and cooperation. They will be lucky love and harmonious in marriage.

Rob Wealth Goat Blade 劫財羊刃
Xin Hai 辛亥 (Metal Pig) + Geng Xu 庚戌 (Metal Dog)

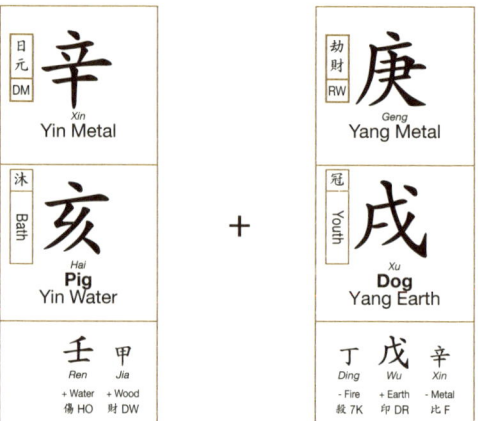

If you are a Xin Hai, you do not want to see an additional Geng Xu 庚戌 Pillar in your Chart. This will form a Rob Wealth Goat Blade 劫財羊刃 formation, which is an indication of serious financial losses and emotional or relationship problems. People who have this configuration in their Chart may find that they work to exhaustion in pursuit of goals that seem unachievable. They are likely to become quite disheartened and disillusioned.

It is also worth noting that anyone in the Xin Hai's circle who has this Pillar in their chart could be the cause of them losing money. These people won't be thieves and swindlers, they are unlikely to set about to make the Xin Hai lose money and it is possible that neither party will even be aware that it's happening at the time. It could be that they will be the source of poor advice or that the two of them may be inclined to be extravagant in their spending when they're together. It may even be that the Xin Hai actually likes to spend money on them.

JOEY YAP's
QI MEN DUN JIA MASTERY PROGRAM

This is the world's most comprehensive training program on the subject of Qi Men Dun Jia. Joey Yap is the Qi Men Strategist for some of Asia's wealthiest tycoons. This program is modelled after Joey Yap's personal application methods, covering techniques and strategies he applies for his high net worth clients. There is a huge difference between studying the subject as a scholar and learning how to use it successfully as a Qi Men strategist. In this program, Joey Yap shares with you what he personally uses to transform his own life and the lives of million others. In other words, he shares with his students what actually works and not just what looks good in theory with no real practical value. This means that the program covers his personal trade secrets in using the art of Qi Men Dun Jia.

There are five unique programs, with each of them covering one specific application aspect of the Joey Yap's Qi Men Dun Jia system.

Joey Yap's training program focuses on getting results. Theories and formulas are provided in the course workbook so that valuable class time are not wasted dwelling on formulas. Each course comes with its own comprehensive 400-plus pages workbook. Taught once a year exclusively by Joey Yap, seats to these programs are extremely limited.

Getting Whatever You Want from Whatever You've Got™ Spiritual Qi Men™ | Qi Men Forecasting Methods™ | Qi Men Destiny & Life Transformation™ | Qi Men Feng Shui™ | Qi Men Strategic Execution™ | Qi Men Warcraft™

Call +6(03) 2284 8080 or
email courses@masteryacademy.com for enquiries

www.masteryacademy.com | +6(03) - 2284 8080

JOEY YAP CONSULTING GROUP

Pioneering Metaphysics-Centric Personal and Corporate Consultations

Founded in 2002, the Joey Yap Consulting Group is the pioneer in the provision of metaphysics-driven coaching and consultation services for professionals and individuals alike. Under the leadership of the renowned international Chinese Metaphysics consultant, author and trainer, Dato' Joey Yap, it has become a world-class specialised metaphysics consulting firm with a strong presence in four continents, meeting the metaphysics-centric needs of its A-list clientele, ranging from celebrities to multinational corporations.

The Group's core consultation practice areas include Feng Shui, BaZi and Qi Men Dun Jia, which are complemented by ancillary services such as Date Selection, Face Reading and Yi Jing. Its team of highly trained professional consultants, led by its Chief Consultant, Dato' Joey Yap, is well-equipped with unparalleled knowledge and experience to help clients achieve their ultimate potentials in various fields and specialisations. Given its credentials, the Group is certainly the firm of choice across the globe for metaphysics-related consultations.

The Peerless Industry Expert

Benchmarked against the standards of top international consulting firms, our consultants work closely with our clients to achieve the best possible outcomes. The possibilities are infinite as our expertise extends from consultations related to the forces of nature under the subject of Feng Shui, to those related to Destiny Analysis and effective strategising under BaZi and Qi Men Dun Jia respectively.

To date, we have consulted a great diversity of clients, ranging from corporate clients – from various industries such as real estate, finance and telecommunication, amongst others – to the hundreds of thousands of individuals in their key life aspects. Adopting up-to-date and pragmatic approaches, we provide comprehensive services while upholding the importance of clients' priorities and effective outcomes. Recognised as the epitome of Chinese Metaphysics, we possess significant testimonies from worldwide clients as a trusted Brand.

www.joeyyap.com | +6(03) - 2284 8080

Feng Shui Consultation

Residential Properties
- Initial Land/Property Assessment
- Residential Feng Shui Consultation
- Residential Land Selection
- End-to-End Residential Consultation

Commercial Properties
- Initial Land/Property Assessment
- Commercial Feng Shui Consultation
- Commercial Land Selection
- End-to-End Commercial Consultation

Property Developers
- End-to-End Consultation
- Post-Consultation Advisory Services
- Panel Feng Shui Consultant

Property Investors
- Your Personal Feng Shui Consultant
- Tailor-Made Packages

Memorial Parks & Burial Sites
- Yin House Feng Shui

BaZi Consultation

Personal Destiny Analysis
- Individual BaZi Analysis
- BaZi Analysis for Families

Strategic Analysis for Corporate Organizations
- BaZi Consultations for Corporations
- BaZi Analysis for Human Resource Management

Entrepreneurs and Business Owners
- BaZi Analysis for Entrepreneurs

Career Pursuits
- BaZi Career Analysis

Relationships
- Marriage and Compatibility Analysis
- Partnership Analysis

General Public
- Annual BaZi Forecast
- Your Personal BaZi Coach

Date Selection Consultation

- Marriage Date Selection
- Caesarean Birth Date Selection
- House-Moving Date Selection
- Renovation and Groundbreaking Dates
- Signing of Contracts
- Official Openings
- Product Launches

Qi Men Dun Jia Consultation

Strategic Execution
- Business and Investment Prospects

Forecasting
- Wealth and Life Pursuits
- People and Environmental Matters

Feng Shui
- Residential Properties
- Commercial Properties

Speaking Engagement

Many reputable organisations and institutions have worked closely with Joey Yap Consulting Group to build a synergistic business relationship by engaging our team of consultants, which are led by Joey Yap, as speakers at their corporate events.

We tailor our seminars and talks to suit the anticipated or pertinent group of audience. Be it department subsidiary, your clients or even the entire corporation, we aim to fit your requirements in delivering the intended message(s) across.

www.joeyyap.com | +6(03) - 2284 8080

CHINESE METAPHYSICS REFERENCE SERIES

The Chinese Metaphysics Reference Series is a collection of reference texts, source material, and educational textbooks to be used as supplementary guides by scholars, students, researchers, teachers and practitioners of Chinese Metaphysics.

These comprehensive and structured books provide fast, easy reference to aid in the study and practice of various Chinese Metaphysics subjects including Feng Shui, BaZi, Yi Jing, Zi Wei, Liu Ren, Ze Ri, Ta Yi, Qi Men Dun Jia and Mian Xiang.

The Chinese Metaphysics Compendium

At over 1,000 pages, the Chinese Metaphysics Compendium is a unique one-volume reference book that compiles ALL the formulas relating to Feng Shui, BaZi (Four Pillars of Destiny), Zi Wei (Purple Star Astrology), Yi Jing (I-Ching), Qi Men (Mystical Doorways), Ze Ri (Date Selection), Mian Xiang (Face Reading) and other sources of Chinese Metaphysics.

It is presented in the form of easy-to-read tables, diagrams and reference charts, all of which are compiled into one handy book. This first-of-its-kind compendium is presented in both English and its original Chinese language, so that none of the meanings and contexts of the technical terminologies are lost.

The only essential and comprehensive reference on Chinese Metaphysics, and an absolute must-have for all students, scholars, and practitioners of Chinese Metaphysics.

The Ten Thousand Year Calendar (Pocket Edition) | The Ten Thousand Year Calendar | Dong Gong Date Selection | The Date Selection Compendium | Plum Blossoms Divination Reference Book | Xuan Kong Da Gua Ten Thousand Year Calendar | San Yuan Dragon Gate Eight Formations Water Method

BaZi Hour Pillar Useful Gods- Wood | BaZi Hour Pillar Useful Gods- Fire | BaZi Hour Pillar Useful Gods- Earth | BaZi Hour Pillar Useful Gods- Metal | BaZi Hour Pillar Useful Gods- Water | Xuan Kong Da Gua Structures Reference Book | Xuan Kong Da Gua 64 Gua Transformation Analysis

     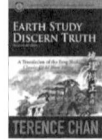 

BaZi Structures and Structural Useful Gods- Wood | BaZi Structures and Structural Useful Gods- Fire | BaZi Structures and Structural Useful Gods- Earth | BaZi Structures and Structural Useful Gods- Metal | BaZi Structures and Structural Useful Gods- Water | Earth Study Discern Truth Second Edition | Eight Mansions Bright Mirror

Secret of Xuan Kong | Ode to Flying Stars | Xuan Kong Purple White Script | Ode to Mysticism | The Yin House Handbook | Water Water Everywhere | Xuan Kong Da Gua Not Exactly For Dummies

www.masteryacademy.com | +6(03)- 2284 8080

SAN YUAN QI MEN XUAN KONG DA GUA
Reference Series

San Yuan Qi Men Xuan Kong Da Gua Compendium

San Yuan Qi Men Xuan Kong Da Gua 540 Yang Structure

San Yuan Qi Men Xuan Kong Da Gua 540 Yin Structure

Xuan Kong Flying Star Secrets Of The 81 Combinations

Xuan Kong Da Gua Fixed Yao Method

Xuan Kong Da Gua Flying Yao Method

Xuan Kong Da Gua 6 Relationships Method

Xuan Kong Flying Star Purple White Script's Advanced Star Charts

The **San Yuan Qi Men Xuan Kong Da Gua Series** is written for the advanced learners in mind. Unlock the secrets to this highly exclusive art and seamlessly integrate both Qi Men Dun Jia and the Xuan Kong Da Gua 64 Hexagrams into one unified practice for effective applications.

This collection is an excellent companion for genuine enthusiasts, students and professional practitioners of the San Yuan Qi Men Xuan Kong Da Gua studies.

Xuan Kong Collection

Xuan Kong Flying Stars

This book is an essential introductory book to the subject of Xuan Kong Fei Xing, a well-known and popular system of Feng Shui. Learn 'tricks of the trade' and 'trade secrets' to enhance and maximise Qi in your home or office.

Xuan Kong Nine Life Star Series (Available in English & Chinese versions)

Joey Yap's Feng Shui Essentials - The Xuan Kong Nine Life Star Series of books comprises of nine individual titles that provide detailed information about each individual Life Star.

Based on the complex and highly-evolved Xuan Kong Feng Shui system, each book focuses on a particular Life Star and provides you with a detailed Feng Shui guide.

www.masteryacademy.com | +6(03)- 2284 8080

Joey Yap's BaZi Profiling System

Three Levels of BaZi Profiling (English & Chinese versions)

In BaZi Profiling, there are three levels that reflect three different stages of a person's personal nature and character structure.

Level 1 – The Day Master

The Day Master in a nutshell is the basic you. The inborn personality. It is your essential character. It answers the basic question "who am I". There are ten basic personality profiles – the ten Day Masters – each with its unique set of personality traits, likes and dislikes.

Level 2 – The Structure

The Structure is your behavior and attitude – in other words, it is about how you use your personality. It expands on the Day Master (Level 1). The structure reveals your natural tendencies in life – are you a controller, creator, supporter, thinker or connector? Each of the Ten Day Masters express themselves differently through the five Structures. Why do we do the things we do? Why do we like the things we like? The answers are in our BaZi Structure.

Level 3 – The Profile

The Profile depicts your role in your life. There are ten roles (Ten BaZi Profiles) related to us. As to each to his or her own - the roles we play are different from one another and it is unique to each Profile.

What success means to you, for instance, differs from your friends – this is similar to your sense of achievement or whatever you think of your purpose in life is.

Through the BaZi Profile, you will learn the deeper level of your personality. It helps you become aware of your personal strengths and works as a trigger for you to make all the positive changes to be a better version of you.

Keep in mind, only through awareness that you will be able to maximise your natural talents, abilities and skills. Only then, ultimately, you will get to enter into what we refer as 'flow' of life – a state where you have the powerful force to naturally succeed in life.

www.BaZiprofiling.com

THE 60 PILLARS SERIES

The BaZi 60 Pillars Series is a collection of ten volumes focusing on each of the Pillars or Jia Zi in BaZi Astrology. Learn how to see BaZi Chart in a new light through the Pictorial Method of BaZi analysis and elevate your proficiency in BaZi studies through this new understanding. Joey Yap's 60 Pillars Life Analysis Method is a refined and enhanced technique that is based on the fundamentals set by the true masters of olden times, and modified to fit to the sophistication of current times.

BaZi Collection

With these books, leading Chinese Astrology Master Trainer Joey Yap makes it easy to learn how to unlock your Destiny through your BaZi. BaZi or Four Pillars of Destiny is an ancient Chinese science which enables individuals to understand their personality, hidden talents and abilities, as well as their luck cycle - by examining the information contained within their birth data.

Understand and learn more about this accurate ancient science with this BaZi Collection.

   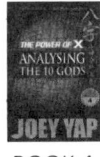  

BOOK 1   BOOK 2   BOOK 3   BOOK 4   BOOK 5   The 10 Gods

(Available in English & Chinese)

www.masteryacademy.com | +6(03)- 2284 8080

Feng Shui Collection

Design Your Legacy

Design Your Legacy is Joey Yap's first book on the profound subject of Yin House Feng Shui, which is the study Feng Shui for burials and tombs. Although it is still pretty much a hidden practice that is largely unexplored by modern literature, the significance of Yin House Feng Shui has permeated through the centuries – from the creation of the imperial lineage of emperors in ancient times to the iconic leaders who founded modern China.

This book unveils the true essence of Yin House Feng Shui with its significant applications that are unlike the myths and superstition which have for years, overshadowed the genuine practice itself. Discover how Yin House Feng Shui – the true precursor to all modern Feng Shui practice, can be used to safeguard the future of your descendants and create a lasting legacy.

Must-Haves for Property Analysis!

For homeowners, those looking to build their own home or even investors who are looking to apply Feng Shui to their homes, these series of books provides valuable information from the classical Feng Shui therioes and applications.

In his trademark straight-to-the-point manner, Joey shares with you the Feng Shui do's and dont's when it comes to finding a property with favorable Feng Shui, which is condusive for home living.

Stories and Lessons on Feng Shui Series

(Available in English & Chinese)

All in all, this series is a delightful chronicle of Joey's articles, thoughts and vast experience - as a professional Feng Shui consultant and instructor - that have been purposely refined, edited and expanded upon to make for a light-hearted, interesting yet educational read. And with Feng Shui, BaZi, Mian Xiang and Yi Jing all thrown into this one dish, there's something for everyone.

More Titles under Joey Yap Books

Pure Feng Shui

Pure Feng Shui is Joey Yap's debut with an international publisher, CICO Books. It is a refreshing and elegant look at the intricacies of Classical Feng Shui - now compiled in a useful manner for modern day readers. This book is a comprehensive introduction to all the important precepts and techniques of Feng Shui practices.

Your Aquarium Here

This book is the first in Fengshuilogy Series, which is a series of matter-of-fact and useful Feng Shui books designed for the person who wants to do a fuss-free Feng Shui.

More Titles under Joey Yap Books

Walking the Dragons
Compiled in one book for the first time from Joey Yap's Feng Shui Mastery Excursion Series, the book highlights China's extensive, vibrant history with astute observations on the Feng Shui of important sites and places. Learn the landform formations of Yin Houses (tombs and burial places), as well as mountains, temples, castles and villages.

Walking the Dragons : Taiwan Excursion
A Guide to Classical Landform Feng Shui of Taiwan

From China to Tibet, Joey Yap turns his analytical eye towards Taiwan in this extensive Walking the Dragons series. Combined with beautiful images and detailed information about an island once known as Formosa, or "Beautiful Island" in Portuguese, this compelling series of essays highlights the colourful history and wonders of Taiwan. It also provides readers with fascinating insights into the living science of Feng Shui.

The Art of Date Selection: Personal Date Selection (Available in English & Chinese)
With the Art of Date Selection: Personal Date Selection, you can learn simple, practical methods to select not just good dates, but personalised good dates as well. Whether it is a personal activity such as a marriage or professional endeavour, such as launching a business - signing a contract or even acquiring assets, this book will show you how to pick the good dates and tailor them to suit the activity in question, and to avoid the negative ones too!

Your Head Here
Your Head Here is the first book by Sherwin Ng. She is an accomplished student of Joey Yap, and an experienced Feng Shui consultant and instructor with Joey Yap Consulting Group and Mastery Academy respectively. It is the second book under the Fengshuilogy series, which focuses on Bedroom Feng Shui, a specific topic dedicated to optimum bed location and placement.

If the Shoe Fits
This book is for those who want to make the effort to enhance their relationship.

In her debut release, Jessie Lee humbly shares with you the classical BaZi method of the Ten Day Masters and the combination of a new profiling system developed by Joey Yap, to understand and deal with the people around you.

Being Happy and Successful at Work and in your Career
Have you ever wondered why some of us are so successful in our careers while others are dragging their feet to work or switching from one job to another? Janet Yung hopes to answer this question by helping others through the knowledge and application of BaZi and Chinese Astrology. In her debut release, she shares with the readers the right way of using BaZi to understand themselves: their inborn talents, motivations, skills, and passions, to find their own place in the path of professional development.

Being Happy & Successful - Managing Yourself & Others
Manage Your Talent & Have Effective Relationships at the Workplace

While many strive for efficiency in the workplace, it is vital to know how to utilize your talents. In this book, Janet Yung will take you further on how to use the BaZi profiling system as a tool to assess your personality and understanding your approach to the job. From ways in communicating with your colleagues to understanding your boss, you will be astounded by what this ancient system can reveal about you and the people in your life. Tips and guidance will also be given in this book so that you will make better decisions for your next step in advancing in your career.

The BaZi Road to Success
The BaZi Road to Success explains your journey in life through a chart that is obtained just from looking at the date you were born and its connection with key BaZi elements.

Your Day Pillar, Hour Pillar, Luck Pillar and Annual Pillar all come together to paint a BaZi chart that churns out a combination of different elements, which the book helps interpret. From relationships, career advice, future plans and possibility of wealth accumulation - this book covers it all!

www.masteryacademy.com | +6(03)- 2284 8080

Face Reading Collection

The Chinese Art of Face Reading: The Book of Moles

The Book of Moles by Joey Yap delves into the inner meanings of moles and what they reveal about the personality and destiny of an individual. Complemented by fascinating illustrations and Joey Yap's easy-to-understand commentaries and guides, this book takes a deeper focus into a Face Reading subject, which can be used for everyday decisions – from personal relationships to professional dealings and many others.

Discover Face Reading (Available in English & Chinese)

This is a comprehensive book on all areas of Face Reading, covering some of the most important facial features, including the forehead, mouth, ears and even philtrum above your lips. This book will help you analyse not just your Destiny but also help you achieve your full potential and achieve life fulfillment.

Joey Yap's Art of Face Reading

The Art of Face Reading is Joey Yap's second effort with CICO Books, and it takes a lighter, more practical approach to Face Reading. This book does not focus on the individual features as it does on reading the entire face. It is about identifying common personality types and characters.

Faces of Fortune 2

We don't need to go far to look for entrepreneurs with the X-Factor. Malaysia produces some of the best entrepreneurs in the world. In this book, we will tell you the rags-to-riches stories of 9 ordinary people who has no special privileges, and how they made it on their own.

Easy Guide on Face Reading (Available in English & Chinese)

The Face Reading Essentials series of books comprises of five individual books on the key features of the face – the Eyes, the Eyebrows, the Ears, the Nose, and the Mouth. Each book provides a detailed illustration and a simple yet descriptive explanation on the individual types of the features.

The books are equally useful and effective for beginners, enthusiasts and those who are curious. The series is designed to enable people who are new to Face Reading to make the most out of first impressions and learn to apply Face Reading skills to understand the personality and character of their friends, family, co-workers and business associates.

2022 Annual Releases

Chinese Astrology for 2022 | Feng Shui for 2022 | Tong Shu Desktop Calendar 2022 | Professional Tong Shu Diary 2022 | Tong Shu Monthly Planner 2022 | Weekly Tong Shu Diary 2022

www.masteryacademy.com | +6(03)-2284 8080

Cultural Series

Discover the True Significance of the Ancient Art of Lion Dance

The Lion has long been a symbol of power and strength. That powerful symbol has evolved into an incredible display of a mixture of martial arts and ritualism that is the Lion Dance. Throughout ancient and modern times, the Lion Dance has stamped itself as a popular part of culture, but is there a meaning lost behind this magnificent spectacle?

The Art of Lion Dance written by the world's number one man in Chinese Metaphysics, Dato' Joey Yap, explains the history and origins of the art and its connection to Qi Men Dun Jia. By creating that bridge with Qi Men, the Lion Dance is able to ritualise any type of ceremony, celebrations and mourning alike.

The book is the perfect companion to the modern interpretation of the art as it reveals the significance behind each part of the Lion costume, as well as rituals that are put in place to bring the costume and its spectacle to life.

Chinese Traditions & Practices

China has a long, rich history spanning centuries. As Chinese culture has evolved over the centuries, so have the country's many customs and traditions. Today, there's a Chinese custom for just about every important event in a person's life – from cradle to the grave.

Although many China's customs have survived to the present day, some have been all but forgotten: rendered obsolete by modern day technology. This book explores the history of Chinese traditions and cultural practices, their purpose, and the differences between the traditions of the past and their modern incarnations.

If you are a westerner or less informed about Chinese culture, you may find this book particularly useful, especially when it comes to doing business with the Chinese – whether it be in China itself or some other country with a considerable Chinese population. If anything, it will allow you to have a better casual understanding of the culture and traditions of your Chinese friends or acquaintances. An understanding of Chinese traditions leads to a more informed, richer appreciation of Chinese culture and China itself.

Legendary Chinese Festivals

Chinese culture and heritage is rich and runs across a time frame of five thousand years. It was during this time that a variety of unique and varied celebrations began to grow roots. Despite China's many changes Chinese festivals are deeply rooted in popular tradition. China amasses a vast area and consists of a number of ethnic groups that all come together as part of a vibrant cultural experience. Some of these festivals have developed into popular celebrations that are not only practiced in China, but also in many Chinese communities throughout the world. Much of the customs and traditions of its people vary by geography and ethnicity yet remain firmly established as part of the country's vibrant culture.

Over the years much of the festivals have evolved with the changes in the development of the Chinese civilisation and as a consequence have become an integral part of the Chinese culture. As with time's progression and the advent of science, technology and rapid globalisation many Chinese are no longer able to tell how their festivals originated which has in turn seen the gradual shedding of ethnic traditions for modern and universal ways. This is especially true of Chinese communities outside their homeland.

www.masteryacademy.com | +6(03)- 2284 8080

Educational Tools and Software

Joey Yap's Feng Shui Template Set

Directions are the cornerstone of any successful Feng Shui audit or application. The Joey Yap Feng Shui Template Set is a set of three templates to simplify the process of taking directions and determining locations and positions, whether it is for a building, a house, or an open area such as a plot of land- all of it done with just a floor plan or area map.

The Set comprises three basic templates: The Basic Feng Shui Template, Eight Mansions Feng Shui Template, and the Flying Stars Feng Shui Template.

Mini Feng Shui Compass

The Mini Feng Shui Compass is a self-aligning compass that is not only light at 100gms but also built sturdily to ensure it will be convenient to use anywhere. The rings on the Mini Feng Shui Compass are bilingual and incorporate the 24 Mountain Rings that is used in your traditional Luo Pan.

The comprehensive booklet included with this, will guide you in applying the 24 Mountain Directions on your Mini Feng Shui Compass effectively and the Eight Mansions Feng Shui to locate the most auspicious locations within your home, office and surroundings. You can also use the Mini Feng Shui Compass when measuring the direction of your property for the purpose of applying Flying Stars Feng Shui.

MASTERY ACADEMY OF CHINESE METAPHYSICS

Your **Preferred** Choice to the Art & Science of Classical Chinese Metaphysics Studies

Bringing **innovative** techniques and **creative** teaching methods to an ancient study.

Mastery Academy of Chinese Metaphysics was established by Joey Yap to play the role of disseminating this Eastern knowledge to the modern world with the belief that this valuable knowledge should be accessible to everyone and everywhere.

Its goal is to enrich people's lives through accurate, professional teaching and practice of Chinese Metaphysics knowledge globally. It is the first academic institution of its kind in the world to adopt the tradition of Western institutions of higher learning- where students are encouraged to explore, question and challenge themselves, as well as to respect different fields and branches of studies. This is done together with the appreciation and respect of classical ideas and applications that have stood the test of time.

The Art and Science of Chinese Metaphysics – be it Feng Shui, BaZi (Astrology), Qi Men Dun Jia, Mian Xiang (Face Reading), ZeRi (Date Selection) or Yi Jing – is no longer a field shrouded with mystery and superstition. In light of new technology, fresher interpretations and innovative methods, as well as modern teaching tools like the Internet, interactive learning, e-learning and distance learning, anyone from virtually any corner of the globe, who is keen to master these disciplines can do so with ease and confidence under the guidance and support of the Academy.

It has indeed proven to be a centre of educational excellence for thousands of students from over thirty countries across the world; many of whom have moved on to practice classical Chinese Metaphysics professionally in their home countries.

At the Academy, we believe in enriching people's lives by empowering their destinies through the disciplines of Chinese Metaphysics. Learning is not an option- it is a way of life!

MALAYSIA
19-3, The Boulevard, Mid Valley City, 59200 Kuala Lumpur, Malaysia
Tel : +6(03)-2284 8080 | Fax : +6(03)-2284 1218
Email : info@masteryacademy.com
Website : www.masteryacademy.com

Australia, Austria, Canada, China, Croatia, Cyprus, Czech Republic, Denmark, France, Germany, Greece, Hungary, India, Italy, Kazakhstan, Malaysia, Netherlands (Holland), New Zealand, Philippines, Poland, Russian Federation, Singapore, Slovenia, South Africa, Switzerland, Turkey, United States of America, Ukraine, United Kingdom

Feng Shui Mastery™
LIVE COURSES (MODULES ONE TO FOUR)

This an ideal program for those who wants to achieve mastery in Feng Shui from the comfort of their homes. This comprehensive program covers the foundation up to the advanced practitioner levels, touching upon the important theories from various classical Feng Shui systems including Ba Zhai, San Yuan, San He and Xuan Kong.

Module One: Beginners Course   **Module Two:** Practitioners Course   **Module Three:** Advanced Practitioners Course   **Module Four:** Master Course

BaZi Mastery™
LIVE COURSES (MODULES ONE TO FOUR)

This lesson-based program brings a thorough introduction to BaZi and guides the student step-by-step, all the way to the professional practitioner level. From the theories to the practical, BaZi students along with serious Feng Shui practitioners, can master its application with accuracy and confidence.

Module One: Intensive Foundation Course   **Module Two:** Practitioners Course   **Module Three:** Advanced Practitioners Course   **Module Four:** Master Course in BaZi

Xuan Kong Mastery™
LIVE COURSES (MODULES ONE TO THREE)
* Advanced Courses For Master Practitioners

Xuan Kong is a sophisticated branch of Feng Shui, replete with many techniques and formulae, which encompass numerology, symbology and the science of the Ba Gua, along with the mathematics of time. This program is ideal for practitioners looking to bring their practice to a more in-depth level.

Module One: Advanced Foundation Course   **Module Two A:** Advanced Xuan Kong Methodologies   **Module Two B:** Purple White   **Module Three:** Advanced Xuan Kong Da Gua

www.masteryacademy.com | +6(03)- 2284 8080

Mian Xiang Mastery™
LIVE COURSES (MODULES ONE AND TWO)

This program comprises of two modules, each carefully developed to allow students to familiarise with the fundamentals of Mian Xiang or Face Reading and the intricacies of its theories and principles. With lessons guided by video lectures, presentations and notes, students are able to understand and practice Mian Xiang with greater depth.

Module One:
Basic Face Reading

Module Two:
Practical Face Reading

Yi Jing Mastery™
LIVE COURSES (MODULES ONE AND TWO)

Whether you are a casual or serious Yi Jing enthusiast, this lesson-based program contains two modules that brings students deeper into the Chinese science of divination. The lessons will guide students on the mastery of its sophisticated formulas and calculations to derive answers to questions we pose.

Module One:
Traditional Yi Jing

Module Two:
Plum Blossom Numerology

Ze Ri Mastery™
LIVE COURSES (MODULES ONE AND TWO)

In two modules, students will undergo a thorough instruction on the fundamentals of ZeRi or Date Selection. The comprehensive program covers Date Selection for both Personal and Feng Shui purposes to Xuan Kong Da Gua Date Selection.

Module One:
Personal and Feng Shui Date Selection

Module Two:
Xuan Kong Da Gua Date Selection

Joey Yap's
SAN YUAN QI MEN XUAN KONG DA GUA™

This is an advanced level program which can be summed up as the Integral Vision of San Yuan studies – an integration of the ancient potent discipline of Qi Men Dun Jia and the highly popular Xuan Kong 64 Hexagrams. Often regarded as two independent systems, San Yuan Qi Men and San Yuan Xuan Kong Da Gua can trace their origins to the same source and were actually used together in ancient times by great Chinese sages.

This method enables practitioners to harness the Qi of time and space, and predict the outcomes through a highly-detailed analysis of landforms, places and sites.

BaZi 10X

Emphasising on the practical aspects of BaZi, this programme is rich with numerous applications and techniques pertaining to the pursuit of wealth, health, relationship and career, all of which constitute the formula of success. This programme is designed for all levels of practitioners and is supplemented with innovative learning materials to enable easy learning. Discover the different layers of BaZi from a brand new perspective with BaZi 10X.

Feng Shui for Life

This is an entry-level five-day course designed for the Feng Shui beginner to learn the application of practical Feng Shui in day-to-day living. Lessons include quick tips on analysing the BaZi chart, simple Feng Shui solutions for the home, basic Date Selection, useful Face Reading techniques and practical Water formulas. A great introduction course on Chinese Metaphysics studies for beginners.

Joey Yap's
Design Your Destiny

This is a three-day life transformation program designed to inspire awareness and action for you to create a better quality of life. It introduces the DRT™ (Decision Referential Technology) method, which utilises the BaZi Personality Profiling system to determine the right version of you, and serves as a tool to help you make better decisions and achieve a better life in the least resistant way possible, based on your Personality Profile Type.

Millionaire Feng Shui Secrets Programme

This program is geared towards maximising your financial goals and dreams through the use of Feng Shui. Focusing mainly on the execution of Wealth Feng Shui techniques such as Luo Shu sectors and more, it is perfect for boosting careers, businesses and investment opportunities.

Grow Rich With BaZi Programme

This comprehensive programme covers the foundation of BaZi studies and presents information from the career, wealth and business standpoint. This course is ideal for those who want to maximise their wealth potential and live the life they deserve. Knowledge gained in this course will be used as driving factors to encourage personal development towards a better future.

Walk the Mountains!
Learn Feng Shui in a Practical and Hands-on Program

 ### Feng Shui Mastery Excursion™

Learn landform (Luan Tou) Feng Shui by walking the mountains and chasing the Dragon's vein in China. This program takes the students in a study tour to examine notable Feng Shui landmarks, mountains, hills, valleys, ancient palaces, famous mansions, houses and tombs in China. The excursion is a practical hands-on course where students are shown to perform readings using the formulas they have learnt and to recognise and read Feng Shui Landform (Luan Tou) formations.

Read about the China Excursion here:
http://www.fengshuiexcursion.com

Mastery Academy courses are conducted around the world. Find out when will Joey Yap be in your area by visiting
www.masteryacademy.com
or call our offices at **+6(03)-2284 8080**.